WORD, BIRTH, AND CULTURE

Recent Titles in
Contributions to the Study of American Literature

Enchanted Places: The Use of Setting in F. Scott Fitzgerald's Fiction
Aiping Zhang

Solitude and Society in the Works of Herman Melville and Edith Wharton
Linda Costanzo Cahir

The Immigrant Experience in North American Literature: Carving Out a Niche
Katherine B. Payant and Toby Rose, editors

American Literary Humor During the Great Depression
Robert A. Gates

The Marriage of Heaven and Earth: Alchemical Regeneration in the Works of
Taylor, Poe, Hawthorne, and Fuller
Randall A. Clack

The Divine and Human Comedy of Andrew M. Greeley
Allienne R. Becker

Teaching Faulkner: Approaches and Methods
Stephen Hahn and Robert W. Hamblin, editors

Songs of the New South: Writing Contemporary Louisiana
Suzanne Disheroon-Green and Lisa Abney, editors

American Carnival: Seeing and Reading American Culture
Philip McGowan

The Post-Utopian Imagination: American Culture in the Long 1950s
M. Keith Booker

Songs of the Reconstructing South: Building Literary Louisiana, 1865–1945
Suzanne Disheroon-Green and Lisa Abney, editors

WORD, BIRTH, AND CULTURE

THE POETRY OF POE, WHITMAN, AND DICKINSON

Daneen Wardrop

Contributions to the Study of American Literature, Number 14

GREENWOOD PRESS
Westport, Connecticut • London

Library of Congress Cataloging-in-Publication Data

Wardrop, Daneen, 1952–
  Word, birth, and culture: the poetry of Poe, Whitman, and Dickinson / Daneen Wardrop.
    p. cm.—(Contributions to the study of American literature, ISSN 1092–6356 ; no. 14)
  Includes bibliographical references and index.
  ISBN 0–313–32234–1 (alk. paper)
  1. American poetry—19th century—History and criticism.   2. Childbirth in literature.
3. Literature and science—United States—History—19th century.   4. Language and
culture—United States—History—19th century.   5. Dickinson, Emily,
1830–1886—Criticism and interpretation.   6. Whitman, Walt, 1819–1892—Criticism and
interpretation.   7. Poe, Edgar Allan, 1809–1849—Poetic works.   8. Body, Human, in
literature.   9. Sex in literature.   I. Title.   II. Series.
  PS310.C48W37   2002
  811'.309355—dc21   2001055625

British Library Cataloguing in Publication Data is available.

Library of Congress Catalog Card Number: 2001055625
ISBN: 0–313–32234–1
ISSN: 1092–6356

First published in 2002

Greenwood Press, 88 Post Road West, Westport, CT 06881
An imprint of Greenwood Publishing Group, Inc.
www.greenwood.com

Printed in the United States of America

(∞)™

The paper used in this book complies with the
Permanent Paper Standard issued by the National
Information Standards Organization (Z39.48–1984).

10 9 8 7 6 5 4 3 2 1

Copyright Acknowledgments

The author and publisher gratefully acknowledge permission for use of the following material:

Excerpts from Daneen Wardrop. "Quoting the Signifier 'Nevermore': *Fort! Da!*, Pallas, and Desire in Language." *ESQ: A Journal of the American Renaissance* 44.4 (1999): 275–99. Copyright 1999 by the Board of Regents of Washington State University.

Excerpts from "The Supplementary *Jouissance* of the 'Ambushed Womb' in 'Song of Myself'" by Daneen Wardrop from *Texas Studies in Literature and Language* 40:2, pp. 142–57. Copyright © 1998 by the University of Texas Press. All rights reserved.

Excerpts reprinted by permission of the publishers and the Trustees of Amherst College from *The Poems of Emily Dickinson*, by Ralph W. Franklin, ed., Cambridge, Mass.: The Belknap Press of Harvard University Press, Copyright © 1998 by President and Fellows of Harvard College. Copyright © 1951, 1955, 1979 by the President and Fellows of Harvard College.

Contents

❧

Acknowledgments

❧❧❧

For reading parts of this work in its early stages, I wish to thank Vivian R. Pollak, Mark Richardson, Grace Tiffany, Jil Larson, Pat Gill, Scott Dykstra, and Allen Webb. For support in related professional activities I wish to acknowledge and thank Cristanne Miller, Suzanne Juhasz, and Katherine Joslin. For assistance with the Dickinson manuscripts at Houghton Library I thank Special Collections Librarian, Leslie Morris.

I happily acknowledge a FRACASF grant from Western Michigan University, which allowed me to develop the project.

For personal support I am grateful to Nancy Eimers, Bill Olsen, Lesley Amolsch, Sherry Opalka, Chris and Sarah Staples, the breakfast crowd, and my family. For her forbearance, I thank my daughter, Lian Wardrop.

Most of the first chapter, "Poe's 'The Raven' and Gestative Signification," appeared as "Quoting the Signifier 'Nevermore': *Fort! Da!*, Pallas, and Desire in Language," in *ESQ* 44 (1999): 4.

The second chapter, "Whitman's 'Song of Myself' and Gestative Signification" appeared as "Whitman as Furtive Mother: The Supplementary *Jouissance* of the 'Ambushed Womb' in 'Song of Myself,'" in *Texas Studies in Literature and Language* 40 (1998): 2.

To the editors and readers of both journals I express many thanks.

Introduction

❧

Of Poe, I know too little to think—

                                        —Emily Dickinson

. . . about the most significant part of the Poe reburial ceremonies yester-
day . . . was the marked absence from the spot of every popular poet. . . .
Only Walt Whitman was present.

                                        —*Washington Star*

You speak of Whitman—I never read his Book—but was told that he was
disgraceful—[1]

                                        —Emily Dickinson

Three authors with the edgiest of contacts: the knowing too little, the visiting
of the reburial gravesite as the lone dignitary, the conferring of disgrace. First,
Emily Dickinson in a letter to her "preceptor," Thomas Wentworth
Higginson, disclaimed Poe in order to taunt Higginson for his literary conde-
scension toward her. Second, a *Washington Star* report of the reentombment of
Poe's body after a bizarre exhumation may have been written by Walt Whitman
himself, in the third person. In the third epigraph,[2] Dickinson again teased her
preceptor by commenting, probably disingenuously, upon her lack of familiarity with Whitman, upping the irony with the word "disgraceful,"[3] an epithet
one might easily apply with deserving irony to some of Dickinson's poems.[4]

The deferrals multiply.[5] Dickinson may well have known what to think of Poe[6]; Whitman probably was both writer and subject of the report on Poe; Dickinson almost certainly had her own ideas on Whitman. All three of these writers were deferred and often self-deferring in their century, for reasons of their sexual choices, awareness of the body, and subversion of patriarchal language. Each poet operates in unconventional ways—ways seen more clearly from the context of the poets' originating century, before canonization in the twentieth century.

Whitman and Dickinson remain, *de rigueur*, the poets to contend with in nineteenth-century America. Though various shorter works have paired them, only one extended work, by Agnieszka Salska, has explored their poetry side by side. Salska studies Whitman and Dickinson from a basis of Emersonian precepts, as does also, for instance, Catherine Tufariello in an article wherein she avers that the two poets drew from Ralph Waldo Emerson's belief system: "Like Whitman, Dickinson affirmed Emerson's central belief that it is the special mark of poetic genius to be able to find the sublime hidden in the trivial and the familiar, to extract the attar of the marvelous from common flowers" (177).[7] Emerson as *vade mecum* may work better for Whitman than for Dickinson; as many critics have shown, some of Whitman's lines can in part be read as glosses on Emerson's aphorisms, and yet with Whitman, Emerson's influence fails to account for some of the most original sections of his poetry, most especially in the parts that have to do with the body. Emerson as guiding principle for Emily Dickinson holds weight when we consider her encapsulated nature poems and her scintillating and complex nature poems such as "I taste a liquor never brewed—" (Fr207). Seldom in the more difficult and rewarding poems, however, does Emerson play a part, most particularly as Dickinson wishes to fragment and exacerbate language, and as she represents female experience.

The predecessor who can help most perspicaciously to see the importance of the body to Whitman and Dickinson is not Emerson but Edgar Allan Poe—the Poe who wrote poetry, valuing it above his other work—for the body adjudicates a crucial element of the poetries of Poe, Whitman, and Dickinson. In addition, the three poets' biographies recount marginalized sexual choices or sexualities, including Poe's decision to marry his much younger cousin, Whitman's homosexuality, and Dickinson's choice of nonmarriage and possible lesbianism.[8] Whitman and Dickinson especially are notable for their nonreproductive sexualities, and all three poets developed marginalized speaking subjects who discovered ways to address the dominant culture. Given their status of minority by dint of sexual choice or orientation, the poets created their works partly in reaction to the dominant culture and, in so doing, developed strategies to undermine the patriarchy. Often they operated on the margins of language, or the sites at which the signifier might disintegrate—a risky place to operate—and the most exciting place, too; I think it must always be the most contemporary place.

Furthermore, in exploring how each poet apprehends language, Emerson becomes even less useful, in that language for Emerson is transitory and vehicular, implying progression and stability; it runs a course. Language, however, for Whitman and Dickinson remains profoundly interrogatory, unstable, and at its furthest ends, disruptive. What makes Whitman and Dickinson the poets they were and are, whom we still chafe to read, is their striving to follow language to the brink at which it disperses, to find, for example, the "sumptuous Destitution/Without a Name—" (Fr1404), that Dickinson invokes. Their willingness to lean to this cusp at which language disintegrates compels our readings and rereadings of their poetry. Not Emerson's transparent eyeball but Poe's sense of the supernatural offers the means by which we can find Whitman and Dickinson's most audacious usages of language. Not Emerson's *Nature* but Poe's "Nevermore" provides the model for redetermining the latter two poets' strategies.

In general, Poe-inflected attributes of Whitman and Dickinson include the following notable traits: an acknowledgment of occult and cosmic forces; a fascination with raw energy; an attention to waste, detritus, and entropy; moments of pervasive nihilism; a fragmented "I" that is constituted by the other as well as by a more conventional sense of a unified ego[9]; an unusual sense of the relationship, notably the temporal relationship, between the artist and the audience; descendental (a moving downward, as opposed to transcendental) awareness; engulfment; darkness and recognition of the moment of dread; the usage of constricted space and opened-out space; the employment of rim and enclosure images; belief in the verity of pain (especially pain as bodily response); a heightened awareness of otherness; a concern as to whether art precludes love; obsessive repetition; tortured syntax; experimentations in sound effects; mysteries and riddles.[10] Of the many parallels, though, one of the most significant for this study is the poets' usage of particular aspects of culture to vector their representation of the female body.

Whitman, Dickinson, and Poe all operate marginally in terms of their cultural engagements and their engagements with gender and sexuality. The cultural facets that can exemplify these engagments include, in the case of Poe, alchemy; for Whitman, the water cure; and for Dickinson, botany, as we can understand it by recourse to the textbooks studied when she was a student at Mount Holyoke. Denizens of nineteenth-century America were steeped in scientific and pseudoscientific discoveries; for purposes of economy, I focus on just one of many possible interests for each poet. Accordingly, in later chapters, I use primary source material to pursue the topics of alchemy, hydropathy, and botany for each of the poets, respectively, to showcase their cultural interests as they comment on the relation of language to the female body.

As critics have noted, these poets' collections of works cannot be disentangled from questions of the body.[11] The importance to these nineteenth-century poets of the female body in particular forms a primary concern not only for this project but for modern and contemporary American poetry. The timing of the nineteenth-century call for American literature, in fact, commensurates with the United States' inception of women's rights, as one-half of a population previously not taken into account began to be portrayed in a new range of activities. With such awareness came an emerging sense of women's otherness, or even strangeness, before dimly or not at all perceived. Along with this emerging awareness came the growing forces of feminization, in the midst of which Margaret Fuller and others announced that the nascent United States needed an indigenous literature. The poetry examined here incorporates the sense of female otherness that in part heralds a new American literature.

Both Poe and Whitman socialized with and admired feminists, and Dickinson remained acutely cognizant of, if ambivalent toward, the burgeoning feminism of her day. While my purpose here remains far from claiming that Poe, Whitman, and Dickinson necessarily addressed women's "issues" of their time, I advance the contention that they recognized female experience, imaged the female sense of self, and attempted to find a language to describe women's ontology, in part the ontology of otherness that has come to pervade modern and contemporary poetry. How lack manifests, how sexual marginalization registers at the breaks in signification, how female resources prove both more meager and, in startling moments of redefinition, more abundant, figure into these poets' oeuvres in a crucial way. Poe, Whitman, and Dickinson poems comprise the first American works to link so boldly praxes of signification to the acknowledgment of otherness.

My focus remains on the difference in sexuality, and especially the tactics by which Poe, Whitman, and Dickinson have recourse to the feminine. My thesis, then, inheres in the recognition that the language of Poe, Whitman, and Dickinson resists or wrenches conventional patriarchal notions of what is female; their consideration of the "woman question," brought to currency in their century, leads them to extend language in fresh ways. Their gendered signification attempts to sideline, if only for moments, the patriarchal signifier, and such deferrals augment their poetic purposes. The poets' recourse to gender in language exhibits not the only method, needless to say, by which they made their marks, but perhaps the most trenchant and eventually the most influential method.

Each poet in the lineage that runs from Poe to Whitman to Dickinson negotiates a relationship with the signifier that enacts the difficulties of social marginalization, and each poet proves an avatar in employing strategies to skirt the patriarchal name. In order to fully perceive this relationship with the signifier, I turn to Julia Kristeva's formulation of the *chora* as an alternative to Jacques Lacan's formulation of the signifier as "Name-of-the-Father." While Lacan's conception of the Name-of-the-Father remains instructive and provocative for this study—Lacan positing the signifier as that which conjoins the previously unindividuated and polymorphously perverse infant with its culture, by the tag of a name—Kristeva's conception of the *chora* offers a way to acknowledge the feminine in the development of poetics. The *chora* generates the maternal pulsions before the signifier, designating a liminal mode in contradistinction to the signifier that designates the name of the father, and affords the breaks in language that disturb patriarchal discourse.

The progression from Poe to Whitman to Dickinson elucidates a progression in feminine poetics, which is to say that their expression disrupts discurssive language. In important ways each poet wrote a corpus that involved a language experiment, as Whitman famously proclaimed: "I sometimes think the Leaves is only a language experiment . . ." (Traubel viii). Poe, Whitman, and Dickinson each, in turn, wrestles with such an experiment; United States poetry written by these three poets between the decades of the 1830s and the 1860s, and increasingly afterward by other poets, is both "only" a language experiment and all of a language experiment. Indeed, the project of writing an American work proved a matter of finding American language as well as American subject matter. Dickinson proclaimed in her poem, "Going to Him! Happy letter!" (Fr277A, 277B, 277C), the experimental nature of her writing.[12] In this poem she boasts that she can leave "the Verb and the pronoun out—." She can specifically disclaim perfection: "Tell Him—it wasn't a Practised Writer—."[13] Even Poe, not usually thought to be an experimental poet, prized originality over and above all else; in "The Raven," Poe states, "my first object (as usual) was originality" (*Essays* 20). Not experimental in the conventional sense of the word, nor in exactly the sense of "language experiment" that Whitman stipulated, Poe nonetheless proved experimental in terms of rhythmic explorations, especially with metre and stanza. Poe asserts that, "*for centuries, no man, in verse, has ever done, or ever seemed to think of doing, an original thing*" (Essays 20). Of course he ascertains that he achieves originality (of stanza) in his composition of "The Raven."

All three poets possess multilayered, palimpsestic ideas of writing, which we observe in the constructions of their texts. Poe revised his poems obsessively, and Whitman produced only one book, *Leaves of Grass*, which he reworked and augmented in many successive editions. In fact, David Ketterer points out that Poe's and Whitman's texts evince a striking similarity: "It is extremely likely that Poe thought of his poetry as an organic whole, much like Walt Whitman's *Leaves of Grass*. Whitman revised old material to bring it in line with the new in successive editions of *Leaves of Grass*, as did Poe in new editions of his poetry" (152). Dickinson's fascicle poems with variant word choices demonstrate a stance of "choosing not choosing,"[14] so that the very means by which we decide what constitutes a Dickinson poem continues to be the most incendiary topic in Dickinson studies. Though this project hardly proposes itself as a textual study, I will pay detailed attention in subsequent chapters to differing versions of poems. Dickinson's manuscript fascicles, which I showcase particularly with Fascicle Twenty-Eight, speak to the development of feminine poetics in American poetry as a whole. Close attention to Poe's different versions of "The Raven" and Whitman's "Out of the Cradle Endlessly Rocking" as they appeared originally in 1845 and 1859, respectively, demonstrate their growing desire to subvert normalizing discourse.

There exists roughly a decade between each of the writers: Poe was a poet of the 1840s, Whitman, at least in his groundbreaking first edition, a poet of the 1850s, and Dickinson, most prominently, a poet of the 1860s. These categories pose their divisions a little too neatly, of course; Poe wrote poems between the years of 1825 and 1849. His most famous poem, however, the one that catapulted him to the status of household name, is "The Raven," published in February of 1845 and reprinted many times thereafter. The chronology of Whitman remains more complicated, as he wrote throughout a long lifetime, and revised even well-known poems extensively, so that he left us the multiversioned Whitman of many leaves that spans the second half of the century, from the first *Leaves of Grass* in 1855 to the "deathbed" edition in 1891–92. Yet most critics find Whitman's freshest lines, his most unexpurgated poetics and uncompromised voice, in the first edition of 1855, which also contains Whitman's most acclaimed poem, the 1855 version of "Song of Myself." Dickinson, too, wrote over roughly the same decades that Whitman did, starting somewhat later and ending somewhat earlier. Her most voluminous output, though, and many would argue her most arresting poetry, appeared in the early part of the 1860s, roughly during the years of the Civil War.

We can see something like an order of immediacy in the three poets. The arrangement of chapters here suggests this progression so as to demonstrate each poet's engagement with the feminine. Accordingly, in the first three chapters, the poets align the poems' speakers with the stage prior to articulation, wherein they search for a signifier or a name; in the next three, the poets undergo negotiations with language so as to discover the means by which they might circumvent patriarchal signification. In the first three chapters I discuss Poe's most popular long poem, "The Raven"; Whitman's most popular long poem, "Song of Myself"; and Dickinson's Fascicle Twenty-Eight, a kind of extended poem from 1863. More explicitly, in the first chapter, "Poe's 'The Raven' and Gestative Signification,'" Poe goes to the birth site of language, the place at which the speaker first positions the self by speaking the signifier. In the second chapter, Whitman, in "Song of Myself," enacts the role of hapless midwife, the male accoucheur, and in the third chapter, Dickinson advances her language experiment by positioning the speaker in relation to the *chora* or womb space, and assigns herself the task of gestation.

If Poe and Whitman figure the birth scene of language—Poe figuring the birth through an absent mother, and Whitman figuring the "I" of "Song of Myself" as midwife in a labor he transgresses upon—Dickinson takes the process one step *prior*, to a stage before birth; in several of the poems of Fascicle Twenty-Eight Dickinson attempts to intimate for the speaking subject the time before language or the birth of language. Poe witnesses the birth site, Whitman accompanies the birth itself, wishing to undergo the gestation process himself, and Dickinson is the womb as she struggles to tell of it. Poe sees. Whitman has and almost is. Dickinson is and almost tells.

Next, in the fourth through sixth chapters, I scrutinize the poets' language experiments and explore their ways of achieving poetic alternatives that offer acknowledgment of that which constitutes the feminine. These later chapters provide a discursis on the process of naming at the same time that they present cultural contexts for such naming; accordingly, I explore the studies of alchemy, hydropathy, and botany, which designate modes of thinking for each poet. Alchemy, hydropathy, and botany—a pseudoscience, a parascience, and a science, respectively—transfer valuable conceptions and praxes to the poets' development of the feminine. Alchemy, of course, claims mystical roots; the water cure has its basis in science as well as practical applications; and botany remains an established science. The three disciplines run the gamut from magic to midwifery to morphology, extending ideas about birth for each author, and allowing each in his or her way to claim the feminine. The three disciplines investigated here afford historical backing for the development of each writer's method of signification, the parallels remaining not always direct but often associative.

The influences I explore are highly specific—alchemy, hydropathy, and botany as they existed in nineteenth-century ideology and as they concern, respectively, Poe, Whitman, and Dickinson. Each cultural influence can be seen at least in part as a metaphor for birth: alchemy offers the terms of regeneration, hydropathy depends oftentimes upon creating a liquid generative space, and botany presents graphic representations of the procreative process. The three poets concern themselves with signification as it mirrors these different processes of regeneration; in the naming described in these chapters, the poets each discover a cultural corollary that serves to corroborate and exemplify a matrilineal system of naming that interrogates more conventional ways of naming. Poe's interest in alchemy, for example, highlights his beliefs in transmutation and regeneration, beliefs that underlie his characteristic interchanging of women's names in his poetry. Whitman's espousal of the water cure underlies his involvement with midwifery and childbirth as well as his attraction to immersion as a process by which one finds feminine language. Dickinson's study of botany provides her with an erotic feminine vocabulary and allows a basis for developing a fresh kind of female naming. Each of these sciences provides a cultural prototype for the language constructs of the three writers.

For instance, in Chapter 4, I consult primary sources on alchemy, such as D'israeli's 1823 *Curiosities of Literature* and Godwin's 1835 *Lives of the Necromancers*, to which Poe had access. To this effect, Chapter 4, "Word, Birth, and Alchemy," displays Poe's oscillation between life and death in the way that alchemy embraces and defines such oscillation. The poetry poises between life and death in order to effect regeneration of women characters, and to allow the speaker to transmute the names of these women. Chapter 5, "Word, Birth, and the Water Cure," examines how Whitman adjusts his poetic program to account for the maternal mode that can subvert discourse. I consult sources on hydropathy, such as the *Water-Cure Journal*, to contextualize Whitman's notion of the maternal "float." In such contemporaneous publications, Whitman read reports of women's labor and childbirth, and most likely incorporated them into his fluid sense of parturition and the development of his speaker as a "mother man." Chapter 6, "Word, Birth, and Dickinson's Botany Texts," subordinates the patriarchal signifier to the maternal sites before the name, as Dickinson's inquiry into biology in general and botany in particular clarifies her relation to classifying and naming. In order to demonstrate this relationship I examine her botany textbooks, such as Alphonso Wood's *A Class-book of Botany* and Almira Lincoln's *Familiar Lectures on Botany*, both of which provided an important basis for Dickinson's studies at Mount Holyoke. Both textbooks teem with sources for Dickinson's female eroticism, and display a basis for the peculiar Dickinsonian understanding of naming—of how names attach to items, such as flowers and legumes. While all of the chapters by and large offer a critique of patriarchal naming, the concentration on botany and the forces of nature in the last section of the sixth chapter afford a glimpse of an alternative method of articulation. The concluding chapter, then, focuses on alternative feminine expression in the three poets' works as such expression registers for successive generations of readers.

Poe, Whitman, and Dickinson each recognize the force of the feminine differently: Poe's recognition of women is substitutional, transmuted; Whitman's recognition is ecstatic (and, it must be said, vexed—his parataxic listings of male and female do not always promote parity); Dickinson's recognition is wry, and also sometimes *jouissant*. Poe registers his recognition of the feminine by displacement of female to female signifier. Whitman registers his in liquid and pulsing repetition. Dickinson vectors her recognition of the feminine in celebrations of the paradoxical yet joyful biological, the maternal principle whereby a thing exceeds its name. For my purposes, the focus for all three poets remains parturitive, highlighting respites from patriarchal signification that can renew the poem and as such propose a maternal economy turning, and perhaps at moments, overturning, patriarchal signification.

I wish to clarify that my purpose is not merely to point out and ensconce birth metaphors. The use of tropes of birth constitutes a technique of writers from Homer to the present and, as practiced by patriarchal writers, may well indicate the desire to subjugate to traditionally male activities the female activity of birthing. Such an investigation of parturitive metaphors can prove enormously useful, as has Stephanie Smith's *Conceived by Liberty*, a study of American birth as rendered by both male and female writers. My interest, however, remains in language as it discovers maternal possibilities that can undermine patriarchal discourse. Robbie Pfeufer Kahn, in *Bearing Meaning*, asserts that patriarchal texts attack, neglect, and appropriate the female body: "They attribute male gender to the world of the above; they steal away generativity and nurturance and bestow it upon the male; and they draw upon the maternal body for metaphors" (4).[15] In contraposition to the patriarchal appropriations of female embodied experience, or birth metaphors, I offer my study, and though birth figurations will necessarily appear in the discussion to follow, I examine more intensively the disruptions of language that allow for feminine subversion. The maternity that is crucial to this study remains that which betokens the drives and pulsions registered by the female body; such maternity holds the possibility of verity because discourse, linear and relegated to diachronic time, suspends for a moment its dictates, to open into what some theorists such as Kristeva recognize as maternal time.

The possibility of a feminine poetics, occluded by the linear representation of language but opening out in its ruptures, provides the impetus and inspiration for this discussion of signification. The poetries of Poe, Whitman, and Dickinson stand as exemplary works by which to explore such an impetus, largely because of the alternative choices these works display. The poets' nonreproductive sexualities and their heightened awareness of gendering and cross-gendering afford a complex and useful acknowledgment of what constitutes the female. Carroll Smith-Rosenberg asserts that "we must recognize and account for the diversity of sexual attitudes during the nineteenth century: the bitterness of the century's sexual debates, the antistructural, at times almost whimsical character of some forms of nineteenth-century experimentation" (316). The three poets here offer diverse, antistructural, and even whimsical sexualities from which to launch three forums of poetry that prove often feminine and highly experimental. Their parturitions incorporate the birth site of language, discovering a female naming that upsets and resets the economy of signifiers.

CHAPTER 1

Poe's "The Raven" and Gestative Signification

❧❧❧

The case for Poe: a little bit the odd man out, he seems the least obvious choice of the three poets studied here. Whitman has often been the most proclaimed poet of his century, and the proponents for Dickinson have argued her, deservedly, into the canon, so that by now Whitman and Dickinson have become conjoined as the undeniable grandfather and grandmother of modern American poetry. In fact, so obvious is their pairing that we might be somewhat nonplused that few major studies considering the two poets together have been launched. Only Agnieszka Salska's work, *Walt Whitman and Emily Dickinson: Poetry of the Central Consciousness*, offers a book-length pairing, assuming Ralph Waldo Emerson as the guiding inspiration of the two poetries.[1] As much as Emerson deserves our acknowledgment, it becomes amply clear that Whitman and Dickinson each inhabit a body of work very different from Emerson.[2] And Poe can lead us there.

Indeed, Renza understands the long prose-poem *Eureka* as Poe's negation of Emerson's "privileged moment when the individual transcends 'all mean egotism'" (77) in *Nature*. Renza explains that Poe "demystifies this moment and instead argues that all individuals (and individual events) exist in a material state of regression or collapse back into an Original Unity which he defines oxymoronically as 'Matter *no more*'" (77). The "no more" of Poe's cosmology reechoes the famous "Nevermore" of his speaking raven; Poe's ideas of both things and language contain a kind of necessary and almost peremptory nihilism. Evan Carton, in *The Rhetoric of American Romance: Dialectic and Identity in Emerson, Dickinson, Poe, and Hawthorne*, understands that Poe (in fiction as well as poetry) and Dickinson to take risks in their art; they both portray a subject attempting to "achieve some sort of contact with, or to apprehend certain principles of, the primal and ultimate reality which lies beneath and beyond the quotidian and the known," and he sees that such a reality is characterized by its "otherness in relation to common experience and its conflict with the apparent, [and that it] is unavailable to ordinary modes of perception or thought" (60).[3] Poe's and Dickinson's ontology finds itself othered, marginalized, and allied with what can be perceived in difference.

I deflect Emerson because by so doing we might discover another valency of deposing patriarchal language.[4] At a fundamental level, quite simply, Poe as forerunner to Whitman and Dickinson can show us more exciting sides of their poetry than can Emerson, for Poe is the more disruptive, shrewd, and risky. Poe took his poetry seriously, considering it the most important part of his work. That fact seems a little odd to us, because he can claim only ninety or so poems to his credit, as compared to Dickinson's more than 1,776 and Whitman's multitudinous productions, and because Poe's fiction has become by far the most famous and studied of his canon. But Poe considered himself a poet first. And others have thought of him this way, too; Jeffrey Meyers stated that in 1831 Poe was the best poet in the United States (53). Eliot proclaimed of Poe's poetry that it ranked with the works of Twain and Whitman as one of the three "landmarks" of American literature (Thorpe 89). In 1951 Edith Sitwell claimed that Poe was the only American poet before Whitman whose art wasn't "bad and imitative of English poetry" (cited in Stovall 181). Joan Dayan believes that Poe's *Eureka* is "the first American poetic sequence, preparing the ground for Whitman's *Leaves of Grass*" (*Fables* 241).[5]

Speaking of poetry in particular, Edward Davidson avers that if one wishes "to explore the intellectual and philosophic poetic temper of the nineteenth century in America" one should "go to Poe, Whitman and Emily Dickinson . . . all of whom form the record of American poetic sensibility in the nineteenth century" (43).[6] It is Poe's poetry and not his fiction that provides the grist for the investigation in this project. His poetry, the above handful of insightful reviews aside, has gone unnoticed at the worst and been underrated at the best. In a recent overview Thorpe notices the drought of studies of Poe's poetry: "Academic criticism provides a striking picture of neglect. In any given year, critics produce dozens of analyses of Poe's fiction but almost none of his poetry; and most essays are analyses of single poems, not attempts to view the poetry as a whole" (89–90). Even French critics have sidestepped the poetry, with their own special Francophone flair: "Unlike the stories, the poems of Poe have seldom been carefully examined by French critics, although they have not in the least been reluctant to praise them" (Quinn 62).

Poe criticism has taken a turn recently, though, and it seems inevitable that fuller considerations of the poetry are incipient. New ways of perceiving Poe have begun to flourish, from Elmer's thesis that Poe's work was profoundly grounded in his culture and "concerned with the social limit" (21) to Dayan's argument, along with Renza and Carton, that Poe serves as "a critical reader of the transcendentalist ideologies of his time" (*Fables* 4). Dayan proceeds to suggest that Poe was a careful reader of Jonathan Edwards, and continues with the provocative observation that, "in drawing attention to the things that in ordinary life do not concern us much, both [Poe and Edwards] discover—perhaps unintentionally—that language as we know it, and as their contemporaries used it, is inadequate" (6). She is not alone in noticing the experimental language of Edgar Allan Poe. Carton offers this perception: "His [Poe's] art explores the human desire to transgress ordinary spatial, temporal, moral, conceptual, and even ontological boundaries, but more crucial still is its self-conscious questioning of the nature, the status, and the sheer possibility of any linguistic expression beyond these boundaries" (15).[7] The initial poet of his century interested in linguistic expression beyond ontological boundaries, Poe can help delineate the language experiments of Whitman and Dickinson. Here, too, exists the poet whose language misfittings can edify, enrich, and thoroughly disconcert us.

Poe offers a likely jumping-off place for a discussion of nineteenth-century poetry that concerns itself with the operations of signification.[8] As Poe adumbrates them, Whitman and Dickinson become highlighted as forerunners of modern poetry, with its disjunction, disruption, permeable identity, and annihilation. If it may seem rash to jettison Emerson for Poe, we must consider that Emerson for all the darkness of "Experience" and his later essays, cannot in his poetry equal the utter immanence of chaos that Poe introduces in his signification. The sheer uncertainty of Poe—disconnectedness of place, character, and voice—qualifies him at the very least for the grudging fascination and growing respect of the world of contemporary poetry.

In Poe we have not only the most interesting American poet of the early 1800s, but also a provocative touchstone for Lacan. Much critical work has been produced on the Frenchification of Poe's fiction and almost none on the Frenchification of his poems. Understanding Poe's poetry as "double-crossed," to borrow the term from Robert Weisbuch and others—that is, literature that has crossed the Atlantic to Europe (in Poe's case, France) and back again—helps us to see the sophistication of Edgar Allan Poe's use of language. We can import from France an already exported Poe to show us a contending

American poet. In a way Poe proves always already exported; that is to say, otherworldly. If murky or obscure he is nonetheless unceasingly attentive to the process of signification, and the French have understood that much better than we.[9] Francophiles have preserved the more idiosyncratic Poe for us until we were ready to reclaim him. American critics have been quick on the uptake in transferring Francophile values to the tales—quick on the tales relative to the poems, that is—toward which we've been laggard. The fact that Poe's work inspired Lacan's disquisitions on intersubjectivity and the workings of the signifier as it constitutes speaking subjects attests to the essentially language-based writings of Poe. Of course Lacan concentrates on Poe's fiction, especially "The Purloined Letter," but if we make one remove, to Poe's poetry, we see both Lacan and Poe the better for the new perspective. And concomitantly we will be able to discover Walt Whitman and Emily Dickinson anew in regard to their poems' attentions to the workings of language. To launch our understanding of Poe I devote this chapter to an exploration of his most infamous and enduring poem.

In "The Raven," the prominence of the mother becomes evident as we percieve that Poe depicts the birth site of language. The raven functions as the Lacanian father who would teach the narrator the saying of the word but, equally important, the bust of Pallas Athena functions as the mother. Not the mother per se, but the figure for the mother, the bust of Pallas recalls to the narrator the undifferentiated bliss or *jouissance* before language, and reminds him of the mother's absent presence. While the bust of Pallas does not enter the poem until about a third of the way through, it plays nonetheless a crucial role in the development and uneasy resolution of the narrator's dilemma. The following section will help to identify some of the terms of this study, especially pinpointing the behavior of patriarchal discourse in the Lacanian formulation of the Name-of-the-Father, but also the feminine prelingual rhythms designated by Kristeva's formulation of the *chora*. Poe initiates the poem by evoking with repetitions the maternal *chora* and, upon the entry of the father-raven, dramatizes the opportunity for the narrator to become a part of the symbolic mode. Poe's struggle between the maternal and paternal modes of expression forms a prelude to the more decisive usage of the maternal by Whitman and Dickinson. As the narrator of "The Raven" observes the bird perching atop the bust of Pallas, his quandary intensifies, and he experiences the abulia, the not knowing whether or not he wishes to stay in the prelingual mode or be born into language.

We twentieth-century American readers have long seen Poe's "The Raven" as glumly recounting one more variation on his reaction to the death of a beautiful woman. There has endured a Poe, however, who offers in the poem a dramatic and exciting scenario of the desire that occurs in language formation. Perhaps modern scorn partly can be traced to an overstrong focus on the mathematician in Poe, the algebraic poet in "The Philosophy of Composition" who dryly proffers the metrical scaffolding of "The Raven," as if a computer had composed it. Such (purported) calculation is anathema to the American sense of individual passion and spontaneity and the romantic tradition of sublime poetic inspiration. Then, too, we may malign "The Raven" because we suspect it of old-fashioned allegorizing, because we balk at a line so broad as "Take thy beak from out my heart."[10] To the extent, however, that the raven's beak can operate as a point or nub of a pen, and the heart as a convention of desire, the poem becomes a more postmodern allegory, integrating in this image the major elements of the desire *à la lettre*—the desire that initiates language. "The Raven" is, in fact, no less than the quintessential poem of desire in language, reenacting for us the entry of the subject into the signifying chain.

The narrator of Poe's poem must gain his identity, as must all subjects, by interjecting himself into the chain of signification—that is, by experiencing the desire that makes signification inevitable, and thus entering into the symbolic realm of language.[11] As Jacques Lacan describes it, the subject is "defined in his [or her] articulation by the signifier."[12] Lacanian desire is inseparable from signification; it must travel through the defiles of the signifier. Perhaps Lacan's most beguiling contribution remains his understanding of how we begin using language, claiming and being claimed by the signifier. He asserts significantly that "the moment in which desire becomes human is also that in which the child is born into language" (103). From the outset of "The Raven," we know that we stand at the brink of such a moment, that we have entered the realm in which Lacanian desire—desire *à la lettre*—prompts such a birth. Edward Davidson divides the poem into halves of nine stanzas each and suggests that it becomes interiorized in the second half, where the narrator "loses hold of himself" and reality (87). An alternative division presents itself, however; a tripartite structure in which the six-stanza sections roughly correspond to three stages of linguistic development: a prelingual mode, the entry of desire and the signifier, and the attempt to resolve the Lacanian-style Oedipal dilemma.

The first third of "The Raven" forms a quest for the pure signifier, undeterred by signified, heralding the desire for language. Surely it is no surprise that the pure signifier is "Nevermore," but the poem takes its own good time—again, a full third—to arrive at it. The preparation for that signifier warrants our investigation. From the inception of the poem, the narrator's lack of a proper designation for his lost love signals to the reader that we start at the site of absent language.[13] In the most crucial line of the first third of the poem, the narrator states that Lenore remains "[n]ameless *here* for evermore" (365; original emphasis). "*Here*": we stand at an important moment, as the italicization shows. We begin at a place where language is unavailable to the narrator, a land of signifier perdition or purgatory where only one word is worth saying—"Lenore," a word with "no" at its very center, a name given not by the narrator himself in the symbolic mode where language is the father, but by the angels. "Lenore" can never be his word. Into this namelessness—a realm in which "the silence was unbroken, and the stillness gave no token" (365)—the raven will drop his one brash signifier.

Another salient feature of the poem's first third inheres in the effect of the repetition, which informs our initial contact with "The Raven" and is perhaps even the first thing we notice. Such an attention Poe would have welcomed. The narrator's desire *à la lettre* starts in a place before desire, and Poe evokes this place with waves of repetitive sound. These waves are not unlike the *chora* described by Julia Kristeva, where "rupture and articulation (rhythm), precedes evidence, verisimilitude, spatiality and temporality" (*Reader* 94). The subject exists at a site where he experiences the rhythms of needs but not yet the desire that gives birth to the signifier. Though repetition of course remains indigenous to the poem throughout, it is never so insistent as at the outset; in fact, here it interferes with meaning to the extent that it renders many of the lines nearly nonsensical. In the first verse alone we encounter the following: "nodded," "napping," tapping," "rapping," "rapping," "tapping" (364–65). Mutlu Konuk Blasing calls the room in which the narrator works—and, indeed, Poe's very use of language in this section—a veritable "echo chamber" (32). The narrator himself divulges that, in order "to still the beating of [his] heart, [he] stood repeating" (365). He next reports the reiterated line and then immediately reports it again, so that he speaks redundantly, repeating the repetition:

And the silken, sad, uncertain rustling of each purple curtain
   Thrilled me—filled me with fantastic terrors never felt before;
   So that now, to still the beating of my heart, I stood repeating
   "'Tis some visitor entreating entrance at my chamber door—
   Some late visiter entreating entrance at my chamber door;—
      This it is and nothing more." (365)

The beating of his heart may be indistinguishable from all the tapping and rapping that rattles through the first stanzas.

The repetition in tandem with the annoyingly persistent rhymes—rapping, tapping, beating, entreating, repeating—creates a din of sonic effects. Much fun has been made, at Poe's expense, of such effects here and in the similarly cacophonous "The Bells." Being annoying, however, is not the same as being inept. Poe may have written "The Philosophy of Composition" in anticipation of just such unfair charges of ineptitude or banality. In that essay Poe asserts that the frequent repetition of the refrain forms a basic objective of the poet, aided by "some altogether novel effects, arising from an extension of the application of the principles of rhyme and alliteration" (*Essays* 21). Poe pursues his effects, chasing sound and not content in this case; "[t]he pleasure," he maintains, "is deduced solely from the sense of identity—of repetition," a remark that refers to the use of the refrain but could be addressing any of the poem's repetitions. Poe goes on to explain that he chooses first sound and then word: "The sound of the *refrain* being thus determined, it became necessary to select a word embodying this sound, and at the same time in the fullest possible keeping with that melancholy which I had predetermined as the tone of the poem" (*Essays* 17, 18). It is at this point that the algebraic Poe can help us, and we should take him seriously. The repetition, intentional and not *ad hoc*, forms a kind of prelingual rhythm into which desire and language might be introduced effectively.

We can find yet another, related reason for the poem's compulsive rapping and tapping: repetition compulsion. Such behavior forms the concept from which Lacan launches the introduction of his definitive work, *Écrits*, drawing an excerpt from his famous essay on "The Purloined Letter": "Our inquiry has led us to the point of recognizing that the repetition automatism (*Wiederholungszwang*) finds its basis in what we have called the *insistence* of the signifying chain" ("Seminar" 39).[14] Freud understood repetition automatism as "the effort to find an irretrievably lost object" that manifests not as memory but as a movement of repetition (Muller and Richardson, *Purloined* 56)—a notion that Lacan appropriates to his analysis of language formation. In an overview of Lacan's essay, Muller and Richardson note that "the theme of the entire Seminar [on "The Purloined Letter"] is that the automatism of repetition is accounted for by the primacy of the signifier over the subject" (*Purloined* 68).

The compulsive repetition in the first third of the poem brings us tantalizingly close to the signifier "Nevermore." Though early on the narrator repeats several times the phrase, "nothing more," this clearly is not the pure signifier; it only prepares us for that declarative arrival at the end of the eighth stanza. One of the seemingly idiosyncratic features of the refrain is that it does not occur until the second third of the poem—an odd feature unless we understand the need to set the stage: Before we can apprehend that "it is the symbolic order which is constitutive for the subject" ("Seminar" 40), we must experience the presymbolic state. We remain preoedipal in the first stanzas, experiencing a stage before the articulation of desire as the narrator searches for a signifier.

The second section heralds the arrival of "Nevermore." Whereas the first third of the poem uses rhythm and repetition, the second third introduces, with "Nevermore," the inchoate articulation of syllables that predict entry into the symbolic mode. The sonority of the word dampens the chattering repetitions that precede it, and Poe chooses the word precisely for its monotonous quality (*Essays* 18). Hence, the term gains effect both from its delayed entry and from the contrast of its sound with the sounds in the previous verses. The narrator marvels to hear a word spoken, "to hear discourse so plainly," and though ostensibly he marvels at the fact that a bird can speak, given the sonic effects Poe creates he must also marvel simply at the existence of discourse itself. That "Nevermore" stands as a pure signifier important alone in its quality of "signifier-ness" is suggested when the narrator reports that the word carries "little meaning—little relevancy" (366). The word attempts to offer us pure discourse, a representation of absence.

Much of the middle section, in fact, unfolds as an opportunity for the narrator to marvel at "[t]hat one word" (367) given to him by the raven. Signification begins to enter this previously language-barren place, and we see the narrator's astonishment at the phenomenon. After all, marveling is warranted; the entry of the pure signifier may be the most telling event in the linguistic life of any human being. Poe is working ironically when he has the narrator say:

For we cannot help agreeing that no living human being
　　Ever yet was blessed with seeing bird above his chamber door—
　　Bird or beast upon the sculptured bust above his chamber door,
　　　　With such name as "Nevermore." (367)

The irony inheres because the entry of the "Nevermore"—the projected birth into language—happens to every human being capable of speech. Apprehending as new and singular an experience that forms a staple of development, the quintessential moment when desire becomes human, Poe's narrator reveals the depth of his amazement.

Repetition, again, informs the crucial position that "Nevermore" occupies in the poem's paradigm of language. We have already noticed the role of repetition compulsion in Freud's ideas of psychological development and Lacan's ideas of language acquisition. The child's earliest experience with such compulsion, found in what Freud called the *Fort! Da!*, demonstrates for Lacan the vital link between repetition and linguistic being: "the conception of the signifying chain," he claims, can be seen "as inaugurated by the primordial symbolization (made manifest in the game *Fort! Da!*, which Freud revealed as lying at the origin of the repetition compulsion); this chain develops in accordance with logical links whose grasp on that which is to be signified . . . operates through the effects of the signifier . . ." (215). Freud first observed the *Fort! Da!* game when his grandson repeatedly played a version of peek-a-boo by throwing a spool at the end of a string over the edge of his cot, then pulling the spool by the string back to himself. When the spool was out of sight he let out a sound, "o-o-o-o-o," which Freud and the child's mother both interpreted as his attempt to say the German word "*fort*," which means "gone." Once he pulled the spool back to himself he would happily pronounce, "*da*," German for "here." Freud reports that "[t]his, then, was the complete game—disappearance and return" (Muller and Richardson, *Purloined* 79).[15] The boy would repeat his *Fort! Da!* game compulsively when out of the company of his mother, which Freud understood as a way to tolerate her absence.

In the *Fort! Da!* game Lacan sees a paradigm for the rise of language, which he describes as a "presence made of absence" (65). In this way the beginnings of language and of desire are coeval: "These are the games of occultation which Freud, in a flash of genius, revealed to us so that we might recognize [in] them the moment in which desire becomes human is also that in which the child is born into language" (103). Before language, the infant feels a wholeness and boundlessness and union with the mother experienced as undifferentiated drives, but upon discerning the mother's absence, s/he becomes aware of lack and replaces the drives with desire. The child apprehends this lack as the "want-to-be" ("*manque-à-être*"); because the child wants to be one with the mother, s/he knows a "want of being" (Muller and Richardson, *Lacan* 22). The moment of want-to-be, the desire for the absent mother, announces the need for language. Only with the signifier can the child move from unexpressed drives to the articulation of desire that language comprises. The *Fort! Da!* game marks the child's desire *à la lettre*, the entry into the Law of the Father that constitutes the symbolic mode of language.

Lacan recognizes the negating effect of the child's vocalization of the opposites *fort!* and *da*:

[The child's] action thus negatives the field of forces of desire in order to become its own object to itself. And this object, being immediately embodied in the symbolic dyad of two elementary exclamations, announces in the subject the diachronic integration of the dichotomy of the phonemes, who synchronic structure existing language offers to his assimilation; moreover, the child begins to become engaged in the system of the concrete discourse of the environment, by reproducing more or less approximately in his *Fort!* and in his *Da!* the vocables he receives from it. (103)

Poe's signifier, "Nevermore," owns exactly the dichotomous relationship between its parts "never" and "more" as *Fort!* and *Da!*, and it in fact closely approximates the sense of the dichotomy Lacan describes. "Never" incorporates the idea of "gone" in an absolute and dramatic way, while "more" attempts to recall the absent figure back to presence.[16] Poe's insistence that he selected "Nevermore" for its sound, especially prizing the long "o" as "the most sonorous vowel" (*Essays* 18), further suggests that the word bears for him the inchoative property—the play of barely meaning phonemes—that Lacan found necessary to the *Fort! Da!* game. One might go so far as to say that the quintessential site of "The Raven" is the Lacanian point of want-to-be, where a human being, through desire, stands poised to enter the signifying chain. Lacan's notion of desire begins with the kind of absent presence that the word "Nevermore" indicates. As the child does with *Fort! Da!* so does the narrator with "Nevermore": repeating the phonemes that make absence bearable, both play out their want-to-be; Poe's refrain evidences the dynamic of the subject struggling to be born into the signifying chain.

Through the signifier "Nevermore" we can find a connection with the signifier of the purloined letter in the short story Lacan thought worthy of such concentrated attention—a connection that strengthens the resonance between nineteenth-century author and postmodern theorist. The "Nevermore" behaves like the purloined letter: it indicates the positioning of subjects. The signifier "Nevermore," from the time it is spoken, defines the subject placement of the narrator; in Lacan's words, "the itinerary of the signifier" forms "the decisive orientation [of] the subject" ("Seminar" 40). Like the signifier in "The Purloined Letter" that governs the placement of the subject, the signifier in "The Raven" casts the signifying nets by which the characters receive their identity. The "insistence of the signifying chain" inheres in the power to determine intersubjectivity, for which, Muller and Richardson note, the "pivot is the 'pure signifier' of the 'purloined letter' that accounts for the automatism of repetition" (*Purloined* 62; quoting Lacan). In other words, upon the signifier turn the relationalities that establish intersubjectivities, or the ways subjects become positioned in regard to each other; also, the desire that demands language demands repetition because the very nature of the signifying chain is insistent.[17] Poe offers as pure a signifier in "Nevermore" as he does in the "purloined letter."[18] The former proves more rarified and histrionic, perhaps, but altogether as useful, if not more so, for arranging the players in this oedipal game.

Of course, we must recognize that it is the raven and not the narrator who utters the initial "Nevermore"—the latter must learn it from the former; hence, the raven plays a quintessential role in starting the signifying chain that shapes the poem's complex relationalities. The principal players are the raven, the narrator, and Pallas Athena—one happy family whose intersubjectivities ineluctably enact the oedipal scenario.[19] Poe devotes the middle third of "The

Raven" to characterizing this family as their relative positions are determined by the signifier. While the "saintly days of yore" mentioned by the narrator ostensibly refer to times long past, perhaps medieval, they also may refer to those days of pre-oedipal, blissful union with the mother.

In the first stanza of the middle section of the poem, the narrator flings open the shutter to allow the fluttering raven ingress—the sounds of which may be the final gasps of the rhythmic, inarticulate *chora* giving over to the symbolic mode (the raven actually emerges from the shutter). With that action, we see the entrance of the paternal figure—the raven—who immediately perches atop the bust of Pallas. At this point in the poem, the gender of the raven remains indeterminate: the narrator imagines addressing the bird as *either* "Sir" or "Madam" (365), and describes the raven's "mien" as that of *either* "lord or lady" (365, 366). As the middle section progresses, gender begins to solidify as the narrator intermittently refers to the raven as "he" and "it." Interestingly, according to Lacan, one is not human, has no individuality, no identity—certainly no gender identity—until the advent of language. The signifier grants the subject his or her status as subject. Just so, with the first utterance of "Nevermore," gender begins to make a difference (and a *différance*). The narrator ponders the signifier of the raven by noting "*its* answer" (366; emphasis added); he still registers the bird as "it," but immediately after recording that the bird "spoke only/ That one word," he interprets it as an outpouring of "*his* [the raven's] soul" (367; emphasis added). Through the signifier the raven has become male, as the following line corroborates: "Nothing farther then *he* uttered—not a feather then *he* fluttered" (367; emphasis added). More importantly, two lines below, the narrator observes, "'On the morrow *he* will leave me, as my Hopes have flown before'" (367; original emphasis). Poe italicizes gender in this case, ostensibly as a way to emphasize that sooner or later everyone will desert the narrator but also as a way for the narrator to solidify his sense of the raven's male identity.[20]

The male gender of the bird is significant because the raven operates as the father in a number of important ways as evidenced by Poe's own emphasis. Literally, the raven embodies the conventional traits of a patriarchal authority figure in his "grave and stern decorum," a fitting description, given that the father's traditional role entails that of introducing the child to the patterns of social decorum. Similarly, the narrator describes the raven as "ghastly grim and ancient" and, just to be sure the resonance is not missed, iterates almost comically that the raven is "sure no craven" (366). Furthermore, the words "father" and "raven" share similar sounds. Even more compellingly, the term "raven" acts as a homonym, colloquial homonym though it is, for "raving."[21] This raving performs exactly the kind of pronouncement of inchoate phonemes that the raven says with "Nevermore," signaling entry into the symbolic domain of the father. The most significant attribute of the raven as father, moreover, remains his ability to say, "'Nevermore,'" a word he utters in answer to the narrator's question concerning the raven's name (366). So here we have it: the Name-of-the-Father is Nevermore.

In Lacan's oedipal scenario, the father's place is occupied not by the father but by the Name-of-the-Father, which keeps us within the realm of desire and language rather than biology. Given the patterns of desire identified in "The Raven," what better Name-of-the-Father could we find than Nevermore? The raven owns the pure signifier our narrator needs in order to be able to express his want-to-be—a want-to-be that pervades the poem through profound images of lack, with the recognition of absence and the loss of oneness with the mother.

To complicate matters further, the father-raven who holds the key to the symbolic mode, relevant as he is, perches atop the statue of Pallas Athena. The bust, which largely has been ignored by twentieth-century critics but particularly spooked many nineteenth-century readers, works powerfully as the manifestation of the narrator's want-to-be, a want-to-be that prompts the desire for language.[22] Pallas completes the critical triangle of characters in the poem's drama of language and desire; she becomes the objectified Lenore—a stone corpse that hauntingly faces the narrator, standing in for his lost love. As is the case with virtually all Poe's treatments of fictional women, the narrator wants Lenore near him, preferably in an uncertain alive/dead state, so that his despair can be prolonged indefinitely. Pallas makes the ideal corpse-woman—conveniently present yet luminously absent. Though some critics have argued that the representation of Pallas exemplifies the killing of women into art,[23] it can also be interpreted as the objectification of the lost mother, the cooptation into the *Fort! Da!* game.

In an important way, we can see Pallas as the Lacanian spool that the narrator subjects himself to losing and finding over and over again. Pallas is not the mother but the reminder of the mother, an object the narrator might wish to make appear and disappear. The "Nevermore," spoken by the raven and learned by the narrator, must occur in the presence of the bust of Pallas that marks the absence of the mother. The narrator's want-to-be takes the form of a *Fort! Da!* expression—that is, "Nevermore"—as he begins to realize that signification signals an end to his prior bliss and oneness. Because of Pallas and the absent presence she figures, he instates the beginning of language that makes desire human. Indeed, Pallas seems to displace Lenore altogether once she is introduced.[24] Pallas is the perfect reminder of the want-to-be, for desire is not the desire for love, but rather the desire to be desired by the other (*Écrits* 58). Given this conception, even the desire for an alive partner (as Lenore once was, we take it), can never be gratified fully, let alone the desire for the partner who, as in the present case, is dead. This desire that cannot be requited is finally the want-to-be that initiates signification; the poem exemplifies how any speaking subject, once desire is loosed, becomes caught in the signifying chain and remains ensnared forever.

In the first stanza of the poem's middle section, Poe carefully sets up the scenario of desire and language by introducing the pale bust in juxtaposition to the "ebony" bird: "I made the bird alight on the bust of Pallas," he later explained, "for the effect of contrast between the marble and the plumage—it being understood that the bust was absolutely *suggested* by the bird" (*Essays* 22). That the two of them appear together in this stanza cannot be dismissed as coincidental: We need both before we can announce the arrival of the signifier. Each necessitates the other; in fact, Poe seldom pictures them separately, the mention of bird often prompting the mention of Pallas: "Bird or beast upon the sculptured bust above his chamber door,/ With such a name as 'Nevermore'" (367).[25] It is not a bad encapsulation of the dawning of the entire oedipal schema, for both the raven and Pallas are further required to implicate the narrator in this relational drama.

Bird, bust, and narrator—the triangulation poses a dilemma of longing and language: Name-of-the-Father, spooled mother, and uncertain "I." The scene depicts the site of desire, of oedipal want-to-be. Lenore was simply a stand-in, and the grief the narrator feels is actually the grief for the absent mother whom the child desires because of her perceived phallus. By Lacan's lights, the child's want-to-be arises as the wanting to be the mother's phallus, which is of course what she lacks (337). Lacan asserts that the phallus is "the signifier par excellence" of desire (Muller and Richardson, *Lacan* 280–81). He distinguishes between having and being the phallus (289); only the father (real, imaginary, or symbolic father) can have the phallus, never the mother, but apparently she can *be* the phallus (or be perceived as such) (Lacan, *Écrits* 289). The bust in "The Raven" presents an apt figure for the mother perceived as (though lacking) a penis—the bust is itself in the shape of a phallus, a shape accentuated by the fact that Pallas Athena traditionally wears a helmet. Pallas, as Lacan might have it, is the phallus. If in studying *Hamlet* he can read the name "Ophelia" as "O phallos"(Lacan, *Hamlet* 20), then it is not difficult to imagine him reading "Pallas" as a similar *jeu de mot*.[26]

More interesting than the wordplay in the current context, however, is the prominence of Pallas in the narrator's relinquishment of the prelingual drive for union with the mother in order to embrace the post-oedipal desire that marks the birth of language. This dynamic informs the third and last section of the poem. Whereas the middle section shows a bemused narrator who can continue "smiling" ruefully at his circumstance—bemused because he has not yet had to forfeit union with the mother—the last section dramatizes the traumatic experience of his attempted emergence into language. In the twelfth stanza, the last stanza of the middle section, the narrator, still dazed, "wheel[s] a cushioned chair in front of bird, and bust and door":

> Then, upon the velvet sinking, I betook myself to linking
>   Fancy unto fancy, thinking what this ominous bird of yore—
>   What this grim, ungainly, ghastly, gaunt, and ominous bird of yore
>   Meant in croaking, "Nevermore." (367)

The cushion, a maternal presence, marks a crucial transition. By its agency we wheel from static triangulation to the dynamic of language acquisition in the third section.

If there were any doubt that the female figure in "The Raven" is the mother (and not Lenore, simply an understudy), we find it dispelled in the thirteenth stanza, which heads up the last section, where Poe italicizes the word, "*She*." This "*She*" reminds the narrator of the mother figure, rather than Lenore, a reading supported by the introduction of the maternal presence in the stanza above, and even more by the description in this stanza of the "cushion's velvet lining." The narrator lies not on the outside of the cushion, as is customary, but on the lining, the inside.[27] The feminine implications of birth space prove paramount as well as graphic here: he reclines his head on the "velvet violet lining" and laments separation from the maternal body, grieving that "*She* shall press, ah, nevermore!" (368).[28] The narrator's want-to-be emerges as he notices the absence of the press of her velvet violet lining, and now he no longer smiles, as he had in the stanza before. Whereas he had attempted to confront the dilemma with humor, he now begins to register the loss of his previous ecstatic merger with the mother; in this last section, the lengthy and arduous labor of bringing language to birth begins in earnest.

What remains is for the narrator himself to try the signifier; indeed, the entire poem funnels to his turn at saying "Nevermore." The final third opens with the silence of the narrator, who characterizes himself as "no syllable expressing" (367), and the fact that he expresses no syllable or, as yet, even an inchoate phoneme, becomes the burden of the poem. Though implicated in the *Fort! Da!* game of spool throwing—reporting repeatedly on the appearance of the bust, wheeling cushions in—he has yet to seize the Name-of-the-Father for his own. He needs ultimately to quote the "Nevermore," so as to orient himself within the chain of signification. Such quoting we expect as the climactic activity of "The Raven."

But the signifying chain has already started sliding: in the eighth stanza, when the raven first utters the "Nevermore," the word initiates language and begins to orient the players to the world of the father. "Nevermore" starts a signifying chain reaction, so to speak. When the raven first announces the word, he claims his presence as proven by the existence of his name. When he says it the second time, the word threatens his absence, spoken as it is directly after the narrator expresses fear that he will leave, just as his "[h]opes have flown before" (367). These first two uses of the pure signifier indicate presence, then disappearance (again, *Fort! Da!*); as reiterations of "Nevermore" begin to point to different, even opposite conditions, we see the signified becoming slippery in relation to the signifier. What was once pure signifier now begins to accrue meaning to itself. Lacan, in fact, understands signifiers as standing not for signifieds but for other signifiers. These signifiers for signifiers form a chain, the "rings of a necklace that is a ring in another necklace made of rings" (153). The fact that "Nevermore" is only (and powerfully) a signifier for other signifiers is made plain by the range of verbal possibilities, as the interpretive constructions of presence and disappearance exemplify.

"Nevermore" itself forms an oxymoron, simultaneously indicating both absence and desire—an antithetical combination of terms that others have noted with eloquence. J. Gerald Kennedy asserts, for example, that the compound word seems "on the one hand to manifest the desire to forget (the narrator will nevermore brood upon the lost Lenore) and on the other to serve (as it does for the speaker) as a nagging reminder of the irrevocability of death" (69). Most relevant for the present argument is Jonathan Elmer's view of the signifier "Nevermore" as both arbitrary and meaningful: the poem, he suggests, is "*simultaneously* the depiction of the subordination of meaning to the senseless and arbitrary structure of the signifier and the apotheosis of meaning as the successful incorporation of that senseless signifier into a position from which it is made to signify *grief*—over a lost meaning as much as a lost Lenore" (205).

Poe plays with newfound possibilities for signification, remaining highly aware as he does so that he *is* playing. After finding the right sound for "Nevermore," as Poe reports in "The Philosophy of Composition," he proceeds to tinker with multiplicity of meaning:

And here it was I say at once the opportunity afforded for the effect on which I had been depending—that is to say, the effect of the *variation of application*. I saw that I could make the first query propounded by the lover—the first query to which the Raven should reply "Nevermore"—that I could make this first query a commonplace one—the second less so—the third still less, and so on—until at length the lover . . . [is] excited to superstition, and wildly propounds queries of a far different character—queries whose solution he has passionately at heart—propounds them half in superstition and half in that species of despair which delights in self-torture . . . (*Essays* 19).

The narrator, who "experiences a phrenzied pleasure in so modeling his questions" that he might receive "from the *expected* 'Nevermore' the most delicious because the most intolerable of sorrow" (*Essays* 19), understands that every signifier corresponds only to another signifier, and that the correspondence changes as relationalities change.

Possible meanings for "Nevermore" proliferate in the course of the poem. The following comprises a partial list of some of the most direct correspondences, in roughly the order they appear: the bird's name; the bird's status as guest, with perhaps a hint that he has overstayed his welcome; the bird's absence; a one-word language, or the (ontological) status of Lenore/mother; meaning, or the relevancy of the signified; scission from the mother; the (im)possibility of forgetting, or the difficulty of separating from the mother; the indeterminacy of truth, or the uncertainty that suffering will ever cease; life (or not) after death, or love (or not) after death, or the yearning to retain the mother and have language as well; departure—"sign of parting" (369)—or the possibility of writing; the nonclosure of the process of grieving, or the inability of the son of the Name-of-the-Father to seize the word. Again, the list remains only partial. Jonathan Elmer suggests that the potentialities of language that contribute to the pleasure also contribute to the pain of the narrator in his capacity as reader: "The pleasure here has to do with the formal qualities of language, that is, its ability to produce effects solely at the level of the signifier. But of course the narrator's pain has equally to do with the formal qualities of language, namely the fact that the signifier's incursion is experienced as irrevocably disarticulated from its signified" (206). The signifier's fluctuations call up the essential loss in language, that the signifier can never pin the signified.

There is nothing fixed or culminating about the "Nevermore"; it is a necklace that constitutes a growing web of identification by which the subject becomes human. In this web the narrator must situate himself by speaking the "Nevermore," a feat he almost manages several times. David Halliburton remarks that though the poem leaves us with the impression that the raven alone speaks the "Nevermore," actually the raven says the word six times and the narrator, five (126). However, the narrator typically reports or thinks the word rather than says it—a small but telling distinction that comes through in Poe's careful use of quotation marks.

In "The Raven" the quotation marks trace the existence of signification. In stanza 8, the pure signifier first appears:

Quoth the Raven, "Nevermore." (366)

It is framed in quotation marks to show direct utterance, a pattern that all six of the raven's declarations will follow. (The original punctuation is retained in this and subsequent quotations to make the pattern clear.) The narrator's retellings of the word, though, take more varied forms. In the ninth stanza, for example, the narrator mentions the word, but secondarily, as a recapitulation of what the raven has said:

With such name as "Nevermore." (367)

The narrator makes a similar gesture at the end of stanza 12, when he again ponders the oddity of the raven's word, ponders what he

Meant in croaking "Nevermore." (367)

The narrator toys with the word, dangles and spins it, but never claims it as his own. The signifier remains attached to the raven's utterance; that is, the narrator says or thinks it but not within his own orientation. He only dispatches. In two other instances (lines 78 and 108), the narrator nudges at the word but does not say it at all: it is neither capitalized nor in quotation marks. The second of these instances comprises the final line of the poem, and we shall return to that lowercase "nevermore" momentarily.

The fifth instance in which the narrator broaches the saying of "Nevermore" constitutes the closest he comes to uttering his own signifier, but he stutters and stumbles over it. Taylor Stoehr, in an insightful treatment of saying and quotation marks in Poe's short story, "Ligeia," sees as significant "the fact that the narrator reports his own exact words in quotation marks only once in the tale, at the very end when he stammers out her [Ligeia's] name" (321). The following line at the end of the eleventh stanza shows the narrator likewise stammering his own signifier:

" . . . Of 'Never-nevermore.'" (367)[29]

Here the narrator repeats the raven's expression but couches it within his own train of signifiers, seeking to claim the signifier—purloin it, if you will—from the raven. The marks within the marks trace the genesis of a speaking subject's own relation with language; ultimately, however, the narrator botches the gesture by stuttering, "Never-nevermore"—a movement that not only mars the signifier but renders its meaning redundant.[30] It is as if he mutilated his game of desiring peek-a-boo by saying, "*Fort! Fort! Da!*" The narrator has not quite mastered the dichotomous swing yet, but he is close, very close. "The Raven" tantalizes us with the closeness—promising us the position of witness to the birth of language and issuing, finally, in a kind of false labor.

Hence we are left in the last two stanzas at the birth site of language, our expectations high but unfulfilled. Instead of confidently taking the Name-of-the-Father as his own, the narrator has ended up only taking the Name-of-the-Father in vain. In the antepenultimate stanza, he exhorts the bird to depart and demands particularly, "Leave no black plume as a token of that lie thy soul hath spoken!" (369). What we might have anticipated as the narrator's legacy, the taking up of the writer's stylus (aptly figured, in light of Poe's style, by the black plume), becomes the legacy the narrator refuses altogether. The word that might have passed from father to son is denied by the narrator. The pungency of this scenario informs the otherwise slightly silly line, "'Take thy beak from out my heart, and take thy form from off my door!'" (369), which, given the workings of the narrator's desire *à la lettre*, renders the line a climax—and a stunning one at that, operating against all expectations.[31]

The last stanza leaves the narrator in the raven's shadow. Pallas is there, the Name-of-the-Father is there, and the narrator, who has failed to claim the signifier, exists merely as the wraith of a narrator. An electrifying stillness characterizes this scene: the dynamism we come to expect from the oedipal scenario has subsided to an excruciating passivity; all the kinetic workings of language formation have lapsed into a half-life of shadow and stillness. Every activity has been undertaken to facilitate the narrator's entry into language, and all that remains is for him to say the word. But he does not, or cannot. Instead, the stillness of the scene testifies to the stillbirth of language:

And the Raven, never flitting, still is sitting, *still* is sitting
   On the pallid bust of Pallas just above my chamber door;
   And his eyes have all the seeming of a demon's that is dreaming,
   And the lamp-light o'er him streaming throws his shadow on the floor;
   And my soul from out that shadow that lies floating on the floor
      Shall be lifted—nevermore! (369)

The raven-father literally overshadows the narrator. Nothing moves; no one stirs. Again, the logical move—the only move—at this juncture is for the narrator to report his own declaration of the signifier, to take possession. And he almost does. It is the biggest joke in the poem—the last word is "Nevermore," but simply, and without the fanfare of capitalization or quotation: nevermore. Poe leaves the narrator, silent, as a shade of the father.

Just as Poe's composition of death and absence is a kind of decomposition, so his birth of language is a kind of stillbirth.[32] The signifier is always already stillborn in "The Raven." The characters are all "still" there, both unmoving and soundless—the pun catches up in its two meanings the sense of the language scenario that can go no further because of the narrator's refusal or inability to say the word. What the raven says negates and reconstitutes the narrator along the signifying chain. He can attain positioning only by speaking the word himself, by breaking the stillness. He must relinquish primordial union, that *jouissance* with the mother, in order to gain the Name-of-the-Father, the "Law of desire," so that he can articulate his want-to-be, but his attempt is *faux*. The narrator's desire *à la lettre* has taken us this far, to the ledge of the signifier. It is here that Poe leaves us—on the cusp of the quoting of the "Nevermore."

CHAPTER 2

Whitman's "Song of Myself" and Gestative Signification

Whitman's friend, the early environmentalist John Burroughs, named Whitman a "mother man." Burroughs emphasized repeatedly Whitman's maternal qualities in his portrait of the poet, *Whitman: A Study*, noticing the reports from other sources as well, such as a "lady in the West," who "spoke of [Whitman's] 'great mother-nature,' " (56) to which Burroughs added that "this feminine mood or attitude might be dwelt upon at much length in considering his poems" (56–57). He detailed as well the observations of a correspondent in the *New York Herald*: " '[Whitman's] devotion surpassed the devotion of woman'" (46). Though perceiving Whitman as preeminently manly, Burroughs also believed his maternal attributes contributed in a cogent way to understanding the poet's personality and work; with the term "mother man," he called attention to Whitman's nurturing impulses and, of course, Whitman possessed many, as evidenced, for example, in the nursing abilities he brought to Civil War hospitals.

As crucial to Whitman's maternity, however, is his relationship with gestation and parturition, with the unborn and the aborning, the beginning phases of motherhood. Whitman himself commented,

There is something in my nature furtive like an old hen! You see a hen wandering up and down a hedgerow, looking apparently quite unconcerned, but presently she finds a concealed spot, and furtively lays an egg, and comes away as though nothing had happened! That is how I felt in writing *Leaves of Grass*. (Kaplan 18)

This response is most often cited to show the author's sly nature, but more crucially it denotes Whitman's use of the language of birth to exceed the bounds of the symbolic by transgressing into the mode of the semiotic; with the language of birth he establishes a new voice, the voice of the mother man. Whitman involved himself in a "language experiment" (as he called *Leaves of Grass*) dependent upon the figuration of parturition. The act of parturition is concealed from his audience because of its inability or unwillingness to perceive his taking on the mother role; he can come away "as if nothing had happened!" because the threshold of the signified, by dint of gender, prevents his full entry. The entire progression of "Song of Myself" encodes a process of gestation, the clues intercalated "furtively" into Whitman's long lines: the need for items to pass "through" the speaker, the "spread" of his body that the speaker notes along with the luscious "lot of me," the "delivery," the "obstetric forceps," the "accoucheur" or midwife, the desire to "compass," "encompass," "carry," "contain," "conceive," and many more.[1] These images give new meaning to the words often used to describe Whitman's style, words such as "huge" and "expansive." The substructure and, indeed, the dramatic pull (rather, in the case of childbirth, dramatic push) of "Song of Myself" depend upon parturition. In fact, furtive though it is, it provides one of the few organizing factors in the poem. Even more significantly, pregnancy is directly responsible for Whitman's sense of voice.

Whitman wants pregnancy for the *jouissance* of it. He wants the sensuality and rapture, the ability to perceive himself wholly as body.[2] Moreover, *jouissance* links the writer not only with pregnancy but with marginal discourse, as Julia Kristeva suggests. Whitman certainly would have been attracted to the pure physicality of the otherness of this signified. He can propound his more forthright themes in dominant discourse while, with *jouissance* as an urge underlying the stanzas, he wanders "up and down a hedgerow" of a line in blithe sensations of the Other. Hélène Cixous ascertains the existence of "the gestation drive—just like wanting to write: a desire to live oneself within, wanting the belly, the tongue, the blood" (*Newly* 90). Pregnancy is not Whitman's topic but the force behind "Song of Myself"; the topic remains voice. His voice, what he calls the "twirl of my tongue," enables him joyously to "encompass worlds," just as the speaker has encompassed the child to be born. Though it can never attain that to which it corresponds, the signifier tries to reference for Whitman an other-status that allows his poem its most charged desires.

Whitman suggested that his poetry obscured something behind every line that "few, very few, only one here and there, perhaps oftenest women" can understand (cited in Kaplan 18). With every reading of "Song of Myself," I have found myself strangely attendant upon a line appearing in one of the later sections of the poem, which may hint at Whitman's ulteriority. The line remains mysterious and resonant to me:

Putting myself here and now to the ambushed womb of the shadows! (1049)[3]

Mysterious as it is, it acts as an entry for me—perhaps because I am a woman reader—into the poem. James E. Miller notes that this line can get lost in the abundance of Whitman's lines, but that it has a startling nature when considered alone; Miller asserts that the speaker gives notice that he will be born again. I think the line may give notice not so much that the speaker will be born but that he will himself bear—bear children. The line immediately preceding this depicts the speaker exulting that he is "becoming already a creator!" Certainly Whitman at times wants to take on the God-function of creating the world, but, materialist that he is—"fleshy and sensual . . . eating drinking and breeding" (500)—he wants the mother function of earthly creation as well. When he puts himself "to the ambushed womb of the shadows," he coopts that female function of gestation and childbirth so as to allow himself more artistic leverage. Whitman must become a parturient speaker in order to gain the specific female power he needs to articulate the inarticulable, which is perhaps the primary program of "Song of Myself." When he ambushes a womb to which he can put himself the result is the "voice, orotund sweeping and final" (1051) that sounds throughout the next section. Through his particular kind of "accouchement,"[4] his appropriating parturition for himself, Whitman can discover and use the operations of both the prelingual and the symbolic; by using childbirth, Whitman can detail his struggle to find signifiers for that which exists beyond the brink of signification.

We can recognize Whitman, so often seen as the poet of abundance who encompasses worlds and contains multitudes, even more acutely as the poet who, as pregnant mother man, contains and encompasses the foetus he will deliver, enabling him to register language both in the semiotic and symbolic realms. So crucial are parturition and delivery to the sense of "Song of Myself" that they lend the momentum of nine months' development to the progression of the poem.

Starting with the famous erotic experience of the fifth section, Whitman depicts the conception that results in the gestation of the rest of the sections.[5] The sexual ecstasy of the fifth section gives way to the thematically concentrated sixth section. Here Whitman asks the pivotal question, "What is the grass?" and offers us cribnotes of possible answers. The grass may represent flag, handkerchief, child, hieroglyphic, hair, and so on. One answer, though, he states repeatedly: the grass is mothers' laps.

It may be you are from old people and from women, and from offspring taken soon
    out of their mothers' laps,
And here you are the mothers' laps. (105–6)

The grass not only comes from mothers' laps; it *is* mothers' laps. Whitman invests the meaning of the grass in the female experience of labor and delivery. Whitman utilizes that experience in order to discover the inscrutable link between death and life. The act of expiring links life to death; gestation, on the other hand, connects death (or at the least not-life) to life.

How any unborn might come into birth forms a question tantamount to that of "What is the grass?" How any signifier comes into being, slips the long ingress from its signified, forms a question Whitman wants to ask of his text. He calls it "translating":

I wish I could translate the hints about the dead young men and women,
And the hints about the old men and mothers, and the offspring taken soon out of
    their laps . . . (112–13)

He must try to "translate" because he is transgressing gender. As a man he co-opts the experience of parturition so that he can attempt to take language from the realm of the symbolic to that of the prelingual and then redeliver it to the symbolic. By transgress I do not mean to imply violent invasion, though I do mean to show that Whitman oversteps boundaries not normally open to men. With the prefix, "trans-," Whitman carries language from one embodiment to another—literally, from a male body to a female body—and does so with a *sprezzatura* so bold that it is paradoxically overlooked. He is a man who transgresses gender so that he can translate female parturition back into the language of the fathers. Whitman is a man speaking from the symbolic realm, who translates from the prelingual back into the symbolic. Elsewhere in the poem Whitman claims the power of translation:

The pleasures of heaven are with me, and the pains of hell are with me,
The first I graft and increase upon myself . . . the latter I translate into a new
    tongue. (424–25)

Using the gestative imagery of "increase," Whitman's pregnancy here is male; he must attach ecstasy to himself in the only way a man might actually get himself with child; he grafts pleasure onto himself; he ambushes a womb; he does it in order to translate, to find a new tongue.

By such grafting Whitman might experience for himself the "supplementary *jouissance*" of women. Lacan designates supplementary *jouissance* as that *jouissance* which is available to the woman because her signification stems from a lack and hence cannot include the all.

It none the less remains that if she is excluded by the nature of things, it is precisely that in being not all, she has, in relation to what the phallic function designates of *jouissance*, a supplementary *jouissance*.

   Note that I said *supplementary*. Had I said *complementary*, where would we be! We'd fall right into the all. (*Feminine* 144)

By "the all" Lacan means the "all" of the phallic function of signification. The signifier of the phallus expresses the all, but supplementary *jouissance* allows "a *jouissance* of the body which is, if the expression be allowed, *beyond the phallus*. That would be pretty good . . ." (*Feminine* 145). Exactly what Lacan imagines would be pretty good, Whitman images in his manifold parturitive figures, borrowing supplementary *jouissance* for Lacanian-type reasons: he wants to push language into new signification, as alternative to the signifier as phallus. He wants new tongues for universes of new ecstasies, and he discovers the best vehicle for himself in the trans-gression that comes with labor and delivery.

   I would like to stress that to consider "childbirth" in Lacanian terms is to consider birth into language. Lacan's figurations prove particularly useful because he emphasizes again and again that, for example, the phallus is not the penis but the *signifier* of the penis. His formulation works only within the network of signification, within the signification process. We can say the same for the experience of childbirth as discussed here; the process does not insist upon, or even imply, a biologism that privileges parturition and hence motherhood over other female experience. It does explore the possibilities for language within the figuration and signification of parturition. To say that the phallus is the privileged signifier is to admit the existence of phallocentrism—to concede but not condone—that within the operation of the symbolic (as opposed to the imaginary, for Lacan, or the semiotic, for Kristeva), a system of the rational, male, logocentric operations depends upon the phallus as determiner. But to consider the signifier of childbirth, of womb-space, is to admit the realm of the imaginary (or semiotic) and to consider what might happen as we negotiate that mode. Whitman claimed that *Leaves of Grass* was only a language experiment, but as concerns parturition it was *at least* a language experiment. No one would deny writers the right to play with personae, to figure themselves as the other gender and then take those characters through some of the most gender-determined experiences they can imagine.

   Rarely do men accomplish such translation of gender, but it is possible. Hélène Cixous finds in Jean Genet, for example, a man who can broach female experience. Cixous notes that "there are some men (all too few) who aren't afraid of femininity" ("Medusa" 289). Lacan also finds such men:

There are men who are just as good as women. It does happen. And who therefore feel just as good. Despite, I won't say their phallus, despite what encumbers them on that score, they get the idea, they sense that there must be a *jouissance* which goes beyond. That is what we call a mystic. (147)

For Whitman it was easy to imagine that men might want to be "as good as women," because women, especially mothers, are so powerful.

I am the poet of the woman the same as the man,
And I say it is as great to be a woman as to be a man,
And I say there is nothing greater than the mother of men. (426–28)

Thus Whitman finds transgressive pleasure in becoming a mother, which is the greatest thing he can be. He informs us that he does not exist in his expected form of a man, hat and boots only: "I pass death with the dying, and birth with the new-washed babe . . . and am not contained between my hat and boots" (124). By transforming himself he passes birth with the new babe; in the same section he further disclaims straitened gender expectations:

Every kind for itself and its own . . . for me mine male and female,
For me all that have been boys and that love women,
For me the man that is proud and feels how it stings to be slighted,
For me the sweetheart and the old maid . . . for me mothers and the mothers of mothers . . . (130–34)

The greatest push for any male poet, of all motivations, might be that of imagining pregnancy and choosing ways to express that repressed desire. Because the poet is in the creation business and must bend his imagination toward figures of creation, he must become aware of the signified with the most reverberations—the signified of parturition. Of course, he can never have the signified, only the signifier, the "mothers' laps" that he apprehends in the symbolic. His experience must remain, at best, something like unrequited childbirth. He can try, though, to push toward that chaos of the semiotic, and his readers can register that desire—a monumental desire. He wants supplementary *jouissance*, and he wants to steep his voice in it, transforming himself into a parturient mother. Cixous offers reasons for the power of the pregnant woman:

There are a thousand ways of living a pregnancy, of having or not having a relationship of another intensity with this still invisible other. Really experiencing metamorphosis. Several, other, and unforeseeable. That cannot but inscribe in the body the good possibility of an alteration. It is not only a question of the feminine body's extra resource, this specific power to produce formation of rhythms, exchanges, of relationship to space, of the whole perceptive system, but also of the irreplaceable experience of those moments of stress, of the body's crises, of that work that goes on peacefully for a long time only to burst out in that surpassing moment, the time of childbirth. (90)

In particular Whitman wants the supplementary *jouissance* that will offer him the orgasm of delivery:

What exclamations of women taken suddenly, who hurry home and give birth to
   babes,
What living and buried speech is always vibrating here . . . what howls restrained by
   decorum . . . (156–57)

This vignette provides one of the experiences of which the speaker claims, but two lines later, "I mind them or the resonance of them. . . . I come again and again" (159). Interestingly, the situation of the delivering mother is one that occurs to the speaker as a resonance, almost as if sound without words. Whitman is after the "living and buried speech [which] is always vibrating" at the scene of childbirth. That sound supplies the orgasmic need for the transgressing mother man who seeks the prelingual.

Whitman's desire for a resonance other than that offered by the phallus that is the signifier might be seen best in Julia Kristeva's description of the semiotic, and in particular, one of its modalities, the *chora*. Kristeva tracks her idea of the semiotic (which she opposes to the symbolic order of the father) back to its Greek derivation, which denotes "distinctive mark, trace, index, precursory sign, proof, engraved or written sign, imprint, trace, figuration" (*Desire* 93). Within the semiotic modality exist drives, including those that "articulate what we call a *chora*: a nonexpressive totality formed by the drives and their stases in a motility that is as full of movement as it is regulated" (93). The *chora*, characterized by mobile and provisional movements, behaves as

rupture and articulations (rhythm), [which] precedes evidence, verisimilitude, spatiality and temporality. Our discourse—all discourse—moves with and against the *chora* in the sense that it simultaneously depends upon and refuses it. Although the *chora* can be designated and regulated, it can never be definitely posited: as a result, one can situate the *chora* and, if necessary, lend it a topology, but one can never give it axiomatic form. (94)

We might see the *chora* as "rhythmic space," then, a realm of sound before meaning, a modality in which the broken segments of signifieds exist, but signification cannot yet sweep the bits into a continuity or contingency. The semiotic stage "precedes the establishment of the sign" (95), and a semiotic rhythm exists on its own without signification: "Indifferent to language, enigmatic and feminine, this space underlying the written is rhythmic, unfettered, irreducible to its intelligible verbal translation; it is musical, anterior to judgement, but restrained by a single guarantee: syntax" (97). This rhythm would be something like Whitman's love for the resonance, the "living and buried speech [that] is always vibrating here [at the site of childbirth]" (157). Kristeva also locates resonance explicitly with the mother's body, as she mediates between the semiotic and symbolic stages. The mother's body, as the organizer of all drives—anal, oral, and death drives—"mediates the symbolic law organizing social relations and becomes the ordering principle of the semiotic *chora* . . ." (95). The way from the symbolic sign to the lawless resonance of the *chora* is through the mother's body; Whitman travels that significant way and seizes that *jouissance*.

As mentioned, the progress through "Song of Myself" suggests the process of gestation; the polymorphously perverse coitus of section five begins a kind of saturated and ambiguous conception that substructures the rest of "Song of Myself" into nine months of suspense. In his search for resonance, Whitman finds the musical, unintelligible space of the *chora* most intensively in section five, when he wants to "loose the stop from your throat":

Not words, not music or rhyme I want . . . not custom or lecture, not even the best,
Only the lull I like, the hum of your valved voice. (76–77)

It is this explicit want that generates the erotic experience of section five, for section five follows immediately upon the expression of desire for a hum, a lull, a valved voice. Significantly, the speaker's pregnancy conjoins with his desire for voice.

Similarly, section twenty-five, the crisis of the poem, depicts dramas of pregnancy and voice. The two—pregnancy and voice—develop together. In one way, this erotic section replays the pattern of conception and gestation iterated in section five, and in another way, it opens new recognitions of voice.[6] Whitman prepares the reader for section twenty-five by identifying himself in section twenty-four with language that suggests his seizing of the maternal experience:

Through me many long dumb voices,
Voices of the interminable generations of slaves,
Voices of prostitutes and of deformed persons,
Voices of the diseased and despairing, and of thieves and dwarfs,

Voices of cycles of preparation and accretion,
And of the threads that connect the stars—and of wombs, and of the fatherstuff,
And of the rights of them the others are down upon,
Of the trivial and flat and foolish and despised,
Of fog in the air and beetles rolling balls of dung.
Through me forbidden voices,
Voices of sexes and lusts . . . voices veiled, and I remove the veil,
Voices indecent by me clarified and transfigured. (509–20)

Certainly, Whitman here claims the political program of speaking for all members of American democracy, the downtrodden and small, the underclass. The repetition of "through me," however, suggests also the feminine bodily prerogative of parturition, especially as it is introduced three lines earlier with the line, "Through me the afflatus surging and surging . . . through me the current and index" (506). Whitman clarifies and transfigures all these sounds, and in transfiguring, he transgresses, thereby choosing the career of translation. The oxymoronic "dumb voices," presumably sounds that exist without articulation, through him can find articulation, because he takes it upon himself to translate a resonance from the Kristevan semiotic into the arena of the symbolic. He translates the divergent, fragmented voices by mediating them through his mother's body, finally to find his one voice. Whitman, the mother man, pushes voice through himself in order to clarify and transfigure—to find articulation in verse.

Section twenty-four ends with a crisis, when "Something I cannot see puts upward libidinous prongs" (557), and the crisis continues into the beginning of the crucial twenty-fifth section. There the reader finds that it may be that the prongs cannot be seen because they form the prongs of sunrise inside the speaker. He must deliver sunrise in an expanding motion from out of him:

Dazzling and tremendous how quick the sunrise would kill me,
If I could not now and always send sunrise out of me. (562–63)

The speaker does not perceive the sunrise visually but vocally. Whitman privileges tongue over eye and in so doing creates a peculiarly voice-driven gestation:

My voice goes after what my eyes cannot reach,
With the twirl of my tongue I encompass worlds and volumes of worlds.
Speech is the twin of my vision . . . it is unequal to measure itself. (566–68)

This voice taunts him and provokes him to delivery: "It [the voice] says sarcastically, Walt, you understand enough . . . why don't you let it out then?" (570).

In the final version of "Song of Myself" Whitman replaced the word "understand" with "contain," and italicized the line, rendering the particular scenario even more apparent: "*Walt you contain enough, why don't you let it out then?*" (Bradley and Blodgett, Whitman, *Leaves of Grass* 55). The substitution shows that he meant the pun on "conceive" in the next line, in which he answers himself by responding, "Come now I will not be tantalized . . . you conceive too much of articulation" (571). Whitman experiences a change of heart in his arrogation of pregnancy to himself; such a moment of uncertainty can only be honest in a program as daring as Whitman's. Perhaps he fears the labor that comes with transgression of the mother's body as she temporizes between the semiotic and the symbolic, and therefore must goad himself toward delivery, urge himself to carry to full term. Section twenty-five concludes with a repetition of the gestative word "encompass," but not until after the internal goading dialogue above gives way to an important parturitive scene:

Do you not know how the buds beneath are folded?
Waiting in gloom protected by frost,
The dirt receding before my prophetical screams . . . (572–74)

Whitman must switch to flower imagery in order to depict the labor and delivery that await him as furtive hen. The folded buds figure the female genitals enfolding the child to be born.[7] The delivery will result in the happiness of voice: "Happiness . . . which whoever hears me let him or her set out in search of this day" (577).

The above sections, twenty-four and twenty-five, reveal the major anticipations of Whitman as birthing mother, as furtive hen. "Song of Myself" offers several quick-stroke vignettes of birth throughout, but none so absorbing and sustained as in the above passages and at the conclusion of the poem. Keeping the reader constantly aware of his "unflagging pregnancy" (473), that condition of gestation that inheres for the speaker throughout the poem, Whitman offers contained dramas in some of his sporadic vignettes. I list some of these below:

The one-year wife is recovering and happy, a week ago she bore her first child . . . (289)

The nine months' gone is in the parturition chamber, her faintness and pains are advancing . . . (291)

[the speaker is] [c]arrying the crescent child that carries its own full mother in its belly . . . (793)

. . . the mechanic's wife with her babe at her nipple interceding for every person born . . . (1038)

Some lines, on the other hand, provide reminders of the metaphysical magnitude of the parturitive project:

All truths wait in all things,
They neither hasten their own delivery nor resist it,
They do not need the obstetric forceps of the surgeon . . . (647–49)

Births have brought us richness and variety,
And other births will bring us richness and variety. (1139–40)

. . . I [am] an encloser of things to be. (1148)

Whitman does not return to any extended evocations of his pregnancy until the concluding sections of "Song of Myself," in which the labor grows insistent. In other words, the poem's second trimester, so to speak, mostly enjoys a placidity commensurate with that of a biological pregnancy. In the third trimester, Whitman returns to describing his unflagging pregnancy, the speaker alerting us that he has resumed his concern with gestation (particularly in the last four sections of the poem). In section forty-nine Whitman presents a scene of labor presided over by a midwife:

To his work without flinching the accoucheur comes,
I see the elderhand pressing receiving supporting,
I recline by the sills of the exquisite flexible doors . . . and mark the outlet, and mark the relief and escape. (1282–84)

Sherry Ceniza targets this couplet as showing a Whitman persona who "marvels at a body that can know the acute sensory experience of giving birth, pain merging into the pleasure of expulsion, the ultimate orgasm, as the persona watches a childbirth" ("Being" 110).[8] As do virtually all the passages that address pregnancy, this one recalls the erotic moment of section five; in this case the word "elderhand" hearkens back to the "elderhand" of God and the other repetitions of "elder" (and "eldest") in the fifth section. Here the accoucheur needs no taunting or goading to get on with the business of delivery, but perhaps the speaker still does. The speaker reclines in the doorway, clearly on the margins, clearly in a reportorial and perhaps even voyeuristic role, rather than as the parturient, active participant. Whitman shuns his persona of mother man at this point, and opts instead for the persona of observer in a liminal space. By the end of the section, however, he begins his tentative transgression into the domain of mother. He begins to be able to "debouch," or pour forth in a delivery: "And [I] debouch to the steady and central from the offspring great or small" (1298).

From this point on Whitman pours himself forth through the final climactic lines of "Song of Myself." His debouching derives from his ability to "constitut[e] a subjectivity that splits apart without regret," as Cixous and Clement describe it:

How could the woman [who has given birth], who has experienced the not-me within me, not have a particular relationship to the written? . . .

There is a bond between woman's libidinal economy—her *jouissance*, the feminine Imaginary—and her way of self-constituting a subjectivity that splits apart without regret . . . (*Newly* 90)

Whitman's delivery in the final section of "Song of Myself" seems as much a Cixous-style splitting apart as any other activity. The speaker as furtive hen describes a self-dispersal that marks the process of childbirth.

Whitman's saturated word "omnific" (660), which means all-encompassing, may provide the best word to describe his male gestation, his pregnancy omnific, in that it addresses as well as it can both the semiotic and symbolic modes. As an omnisexual poet whose language reflects his expansive sexuality, Whitman plays the role of mother to reflect the essential plenary and ambiguous relation to *jouissance* that he celebrates. When he boasts that he contains multitudes he claims exactly this kind of omnific experience:

Do I contradict myself?
Very well then . . . I contradict myself;
I am large . . . I contain multitudes. (1314–16)

The contradiction involves, in part, the contradiction in gender taken on by the mother man who desires the rapture of omnific experience so as to find semiotic voice. It involves at least this: the semiotic voice Whitman perceives as lull, hum, resonance.

Whitman contradicts himself, transgresses gender, and attempts to translate the childbearing role of the woman back into the symbolic realm of the father. His program of translation, of omnific semiotics, so to speak, buoys him so that he can accomplish the disappearing act in the finale, section fifty-two, in which he disperses but does not die. He splits apart and keeps on talking. He does it furtively, powerfully, by claiming supplementary *jouissance*, the rapture that floods the mother during and upon arrival of the child. Kristeva suggests such *jouissance* as follows:

The child: sole evidence, for the symbolic order, of *jouissance* and pregnancy, thanks to whom the woman will be coded in the chain of production and thus perceived as a temporalized parent. *Jouissance*, pregnancy, marginal discourse: this is the way in which this "truth," hidden and cloaked [*dérobent et enrobent*] by the truth of the symbolic order and its time, functions through women. (*Desire* 154)

For Whitman, necessarily, the "truth" remains hidden and cloaked, the agenda, furtive.

I want to offer the caveat again that Whitman's role as mother is exactly furtive, that the imagining of the pregnant mother man intimates a semiotic realm behind and beyond the symbolic realm we usually perceive when we read "Song of Myself." Needless to say, that is the point: the semiotic *chora* can be got at only by intimation—by lull, by hum, by resonance. He attempts such resonance in this way because the project is male and the signified, in this case, singularly female. Whitman tries to experience the *jouissance* that the *chora* has to offer not because, as in the case with women, he has been left out of the signifying chain and relegated to the semiotic; rather, he tries to get there because he chooses to. Whitman chooses to marginalize his discourse.

Is the project successful? Does he make it to the semiotic side of utterance? The last section plays out that drama, and lingers in the uncertainty. When we ask if he transgresses completely, the answer seems to be both yes and no. Whitman's career of translation at least partially fails, as it probably must, given the almost preposterous if somewhat laudable scope of his gender-crossing ambitions. He must claim, finally, that "I too am untranslatable" (1322), a poignant claim given the magnitude of his desire to "translate" all the hints about mothers' laps in section six. And yet he can still summon the resonance, the sound without articulation that heralds the privilege of omnific semiotics, of recourse to the *chora*: "I sound my barbaric yawp over the roofs of the world" (1323). With his famous barbaric yawp he accompanies parturition, perhaps, with a rough approximation to vocalization during female delivery. Whitman finds his very own gender-transgressed resonance, and though absolute translation may remain impossible, the yawp that comes with broaching the semiotic may sound a kind of victory for Whitman in his attempt to find new tongue and new voice.

Whitman exhibits enormous bravery—and bravura—in attempting to find a gender-crossed voice. Of course the bravura is nothing new for Whitman, but his bravery in taking on the mother role has not been sufficiently recognized in the past. Astute enough to anticipate what Cixous will iterate—that women reserve a "privileged relationship with the voice"—Whitman arranges "Song of Myself" as best he can in order to be able to sing both as man and mother man. His mother's voice is his best resonance, and Cixous states this resonance as follows:

In women's speech, as in their writing, that element which never stops resonating, which, once we've been permeated by it, profoundly and imperceptibly touched by it,

43

retains the power of moving us—that element is the song: first music from the first voice of love which is alive in every woman. Why this privileged relationship with the voice? Because no woman stockpiles as many defenses for countering the drives as does a man. You don't build walls around yourself, you don't forego pleasure as "wisely" as he.... [A] woman is never far from "mother" (. . . as nonname and as source of goods). There is always within her at least a little of that good mother's milk. She writes in white ink. ("Medusa" 285)[9]

Once he realizes the advantages of first song, as Cixous phrases it, of a voice that might never stop resonating, what male author wouldn't want to try to appropriate for himself the advantage of white ink, the mother's *jouissance*? What male author wouldn't ambush a womb for his poetry?

The faint-hearted or the practical might not, for in the end the project can never reach a satisfying completion, and must always recognize its own partial failure. That desire for total—with the concomitant admission of partial—transgression remains one of Whitman's most powerful traits as a poet in pursuit of truth at any cost. We see his partiality and love of truth in the final section, as dusk approaches:

The last scud of day holds back for me,
It flings my likeness after the rest and true as any on the shadowed wilds,
It coaxes me to the vapor and the dusk. (1324–26)

The "shadowed wilds" recall the "ambushed womb of the shadows," especially as the section allows him to fling his "likeness," which may represent his progeny, or his book, both of which would be "like" him but not him himself. Such a likeness issues from a kind of immaculate delivery, sparked by the intensively ambiguous and erotic fifth section near the start of the poem. Whitman's marginalizing discourse allows him to deliver this likeness of himself at the end of the poem. As cited above, Kristeva notes that the child is the sole evidence for those in the symbolic realm of the existence of the semiotic. Whitman's "child" cannot exist as the actual child that a mother delivers, of course, so he presents his "likeness" necessarily as a projection, a shadowy and vaporous offspring of a shadowy womb that he burglarizes through the operations of language. The omnific semiotics that he gains from attempting to transgress the *chora* of female experience provide him with some of his most daring language experiments.

CHAPTER 3

Dickinson's Fascicle Twenty-Eight and Gestative Signification

Emily Dickinson is often seen as a poet of death but almost never as a poet of birth. Her concern with death has been considered relentless and obsessive, registering experience after the grave, but her concern with gestation has gone largely unnoticed. Specifically, Dickinson is more than a great poet of death; she is also a poet of language after death and commensurately, a poet of language before birth. Of course both are impossible, but she strains toward them, trains herself at the cleft between the signifier and the void. The site of death and after-death has been examined by various critics; the site of birth and before-birth will concern us here—the realm of gestation. How does the state before birth figure in Dickinson's poetry and how can she say it; indeed, how sayable is it?

Representing motherhood remains a high-stakes endeavor for a female poet. In the nineteenth century, the taboos involved in the writing of a motherhood that was anything but replete, fulfilling, and inevitable are formidable, for to enter into representation of a gestation characterized in any way but according to the cult of motherhood defies the dictates of Victorian decorum and prudence. Furthermore, to represent a gestation that ends before full term becomes so risqué as to be nearly unthought of. Even in the twentieth century, the representation of gestation and the unborn proves relatively rare in canonized poetry.[1]

In fact, the representation of gestation by women becomes, if we take into account French language theorists such as Julia Kristeva, the territory of male writers. Kristeva claims that the *jouissance* of gestation can only be experienced but not told by mothers; i.e., women can be but not have the rapture of gestation. Hence, Dickinson's courage in taking on such an endeavor, given the historical obstacles and theoretical problems, proves remarkable. We have come to expect daring from Emily Dickinson's poetry, but perhaps nothing quite as audacious as the correlation of gestation with the "nameless pod" of Fascicle Twenty-Eight.

Dickinson wrote of gestation not carried to full term; the pregnancies in her poems may have resulted in miscarriage or abortion.[2] I would like to stress that I discuss exactly and solely the pregnancies *in her poems*; the representation of parturition here in no way implies that the poet herself necessarily underwent the experience.[3] One of the primary conditions of poetry entails the exploration of imagined experience; hence, Dickinson could write about being a wife when she never actually married, about being a boy when of course she wasn't, and so on. The pregnancy of a narrator does not equal the pregnancy of the poet, needless to say; it is, however, cogent to this study to recognize that Dickinson the poet was aware of the existence of miscarriage and abortion.

That Dickinson would have been aware becomes manifestly clear when we turn to studies of nineteenth-century motherhood, pregnancy, and abortion, which suggest that the merchandisers of contraceptive and abortive products advertised widely in Dickinson's time. Janet Farrell Brodie, in her *Contraception and Abortion in Nineteenth-Century America*, states that, upon beginning her study, she expected information on the topic to be sparse but "it quickly became apparent that in the second quarter of the nineteenth century information on American reproductive control [including abortion, given Brodie's definition of contraception] was neither all that rare nor all that tabooed" (ix). Kristin Luker, too, reports that "contrary to our assumptions about 'Victorian morality' the available evidence suggests that abortions were frequent" (18). Carl Degler also affirms "the widespread practice of abortion, especially after 1830" (227).[4]

Many papers, medical journals, and broadsides carried advertisements for products designed to regulate the "courses" or menses, and touted medicines such as rue, tansy, savin, cotton root, and ergot, mentioned in conjunction with "'ladies' relief' or promises to 'cure irregularities'" (Brodie 5). While we may not recognize in these euphemisms offers of medicines to induce abortion, nineteenth-century women would have, states Brodie: "each contraceptive method had its own synonym, many of them an obscure and transitory argot" (5). Information on abortion proved so available, claims Luker, that women could read about it, in some cases, "even in church newspapers." Luker explains that "[d]iscreet advertisements for 'clinics for ladies' where menstrual irregularities 'from whatever cause' could be treated (and where confidentiality and even private off-street entrances were carefully noted in the advertisement itself) were common" (18–19).

In addition, Dickinson might have been very well informed about the ambivalent emotions caused by a terminated pregnancy, as her sister-in-law and intimate friend, Susan Gilbert Dickinson, may have experienced one or several such pregnancies. According to Mabel Loomis Todd's journal, Ned was born five years after Sue and Austin married, and "only after Sue had 'caused three or four to be artificially removed' and had failed in repeated attempts to prevent his birth" (cited in Sewall I: 189). In fact, Todd attributed Ned's epilepsy to Sue's attempted abortion. In a later journal Todd again recorded that Sue "'had four [children] killed before birth'" (Sewall I; 189). Sewall responds to these journal entries with caution: "These revelations may all be factual; they may not be; they may be partly so" (Sewall I; 189).

Even if Sue never terminated a pregnancy, Dickinson would have been able to cull and absorb information on the subject of miscarriages and abortions, readily available to most nineteenth-century American women. In her poetry she takes pains to disguise this awareness, just as the advertisements for women's health were disguised (as for example with the phrase, "suppressed menses"). Dickinson chose a variety of euphemisms for the process of gestation, but one of her major guises draws, aptly enough, upon the natural world. Consider, for example, the following poem from Fascicle Twenty-Eight[5]:

How many Flowers fail in Wood—
Or perish from the Hill—
Without the privilege to know
That they are Beautiful—

How many Cast a nameless Pod
Opon the nearest Breeze—
Unconscious of the Scarlet Freight—
It bear to Other Eyes—

In this concise poem (Fr534) that has received relatively little critical attention, the speaker asks two seemingly rhetorical questions: How many "fail" in "wood" and "How many Cast a nameless Pod?" The first question asks about the unborn, while the second asks about the mother of the unborn, and both target the emotional difficulty of the topic and the reality that no easy answers exist.[6] The poem, upon first reading an exploration of relative values and human potential, carries trenchant words in the last two lines, "Scarlet Freight" and "bear." Given that a nineteenth-century poet could not speak directly of miscarriage and abortion, could a more effective means of reference have been utilized? By far the most memorable words, however, inhere in the phrase, "nameless Pod." As if a pod were ever anything but nameless: but here Dickinson insists, and it is the insistence that argues for the poem as one about gestation.

Similarly, another poem, "It knew no Medicine—" (Fr567), presents color and namelessness. Though not in Fascicle Twenty-Eight, "It knew no Medicine—" occupies the penultimate position in Fascicle Twenty-Seven. As the poem specifies that the subject needs no medicine or surgery, it most likely encodes miscarriage as opposed to abortion:

It knew no Medicine—
It was not Sickness—then—
Nor any need of Surgery—
And therefore—'twas not Pain—

It moved away the Cheeks—
A Dimple at a time—
And left the Profile—plainer—
And in the+ place of Bloom

It left the little Tint
That never had a Name—
You've seen it on a Cast's+ face—
Was Paradise—to blame—

If +momently ajar—
Temerity—drew near—
And sickened—ever afterward
For somewhat that it saw?
+ stead + Cheek + Her sweet
Door—ajar + Whatsoe'er—

This poem reiterates the gestation images in "How many Flowers fail in Wood—," and with "the little Tint/That never had a Name—" parallels the namelessness of the pod, and the "Scarlet Freight" of the poem, "How many Flowers fail in Wood—" in Fascicle Twenty-Eight.

This latter poem appears tenth in the twenty-three poems of Fascicle Twenty-Eight, and second after the blank page and a half that breaks up the fascicle ten pages from the beginning. The fascicle as a whole provides ample cause for study, given its many symmetries, repetitions, anomalies, and gatherings of motifs. Some of these motifs include the concern with the nature of the signifier in the first and last poems, the constant themes of counting and accounting, and the repeated attentions to the nature of poetry and the role of the poet. The fascicle configures the underlying and "duplicitous" evocation of failed parturition throughout, the word "duplicitous" referring to a poetic strategy, as Alicia Ostriker elucidates (39); a woman poet, especially, proves duplicitous in that she creates a poem that can mean two things at once—namely, what her culture allows her to say on the surface, and what she must bury, because disallowed, within the poem. The word "pod" exemplifies such duplicity.

Emily Dickinson uses the term "pod" four times in the course of Fascicle Twenty-Eight, whereas she uses the term nine times (ten times, if counting the plural instance "pods"), in her entire *oeuvre*, including once in the opening poem of the preceding booklet, Fascicle Twenty- Seven. There exist numerous reasons for reading Dickinson by the fascicle rather than by the poem, and identifying the importance of an image through the repetition of a word such as "pod" provides only one of them. In *Choosing Not Choosing* Sharon Cameron, one of the most eloquent exponents of reading the fascicles, asserts that in the Thomas Johnson edition, "the unit of sense is the individual poem," whereas in the R. W. Franklin manuscript books, the unit of sense is the fascicle (15).[7] My examination of Dickinson's poetry of gestation and of the signifier depends upon the fascicle as a unit of sense, and Fascicle Twenty-Eight offers a forum for Dickinson's poems of signification that address the signifier by recourse to the image of gestation.[8]

My reading of Fascicle Twenty-Eight depends to some extent upon a material consideration of the manuscripts. While my study does not supply so determined a reading, for example, as does Dorothy Oberhaus's reading of Fascicle Forty,[9] nor is it so visually based as Marta Werner's reading of the open folios, which she describes as making a shift "from the lexical to the visual" (15),[10] I draw from both as predecessors. If we accede to the argument that the fascicles provide a viable way of reading Dickinson, then we must accept that she had at least as much control over the material production of her art as, say, a poet like Blake, who wrote, illustrated, printed, and produced his own texts. Dickinson, too, proves herself the self-published producer of the fascicle texts, making final decisions about copying, editing, layout, font, ordering, binding, and even paper stock. Accordingly, the physical facts of the fascicle remain relevant to a consideration of Dickinson's art as Dickinson herself oversaw the final production.

I wish to examine rather than explicate Fascicle Twenty-Eight, explore rather than adjudicate in any finalizing way. During the progress of the fascicle Dickinson offers repeatedly for meditation the signifiers "prayer," "dying," "death," "truth," "poets," "delight," "loss," "heaven," of course "pod," and others. The fascicle enacts an extended meditation on lexicographical slippage, on the workings of the signifier through the course of a manuscript. Rather than setting forth in the poetry an idea or even a dialectic that we might espy, Dickinson offers an associative discursion that grows with the reading of each poem in the fascicle.[11] Indeed, she enhances the discursion with each grouping of word variants following some poems, sometimes found-poems in themselves. As readers we register and develop a kind of impressionistic ontology of signification that encodes and instates the body, particularly the female body.

Appropriately, Dickinson's booklets of poems were called, by her sister Lavinia, "fascicles," a term connoting the body: "in terms of the body, a fascicle defines a small cluster of muscle or nerve fibers" (cited in Robert Smith 16). This meaning of "fascicle" serves admirably to capture both the method and the intent of the poems presented in Fascicle Twenty-Eight; the poems perform much less as a platform for a position than they do as bodily systems, organic functions and drives, that feed into each other and circle back, then continue circulating.[12] Dickinson has been seen by various critics as predating a kind of *écriture féminine*, that is, writing the text that is the body.[13] Augmenting that position by understanding it particularly as a sometimes gravid text, I propose that Dickinson at times writes about the gestative female body that undergoes miscarriage or abortion.[14]

Motherhood vectors a particular vantage point for considering the act of signification and its attendant difficulties. Women, in a difficult enough place to begin with, possess an entirely distinct relationship to signification, according to Jacques Lacan. As Elizabeth Grosz explains it, in the Lacanian speaking position, the boy

becomes an "I," and can speak in its own name. What occurs in the case of the girl is less clear and explicable. In one sense, in so far as she speaks and says "I," she too must take up a place as a subject of the symbolic; yet, in another, in so far as she is positioned as castrated, passive, an object of desire for men rather than a subject who desires, her position within the symbolic must be marginal or tenuous: when she speaks as an "I" it is never clear that she speaks (of or as) herself. She speaks in a mode of masquerade, in imitation of the masculine, phallic subject. (71–72)

Apparently the woman speaker exists simultaneously in the symbolic and the real; she exists in both but, as Lacan has it, she exists only marginally in the symbolic. By entering the symbolic the boy takes on the Name-of-the-Father, but the girl, while she speaks, must do so without ever truly having the patronymic. Still she must speak under its aegis, as if under an assumed name, and the dilemma herein demonstrates the trenchant problem for women writers in a patriarchal culture; they must be at the same time centric and eccentric, primary and liminal, at the middle and the interstitial. In this context, I note

Cameron's cogent suggestion that the fascicles offer a more heteroglossic reading of Dickinson, proffering the advantage of reading the poem centered on the manuscript page with and against the word variants in the margins, both as extrinsic and intrinsic to the poem.[15] Accordingly, the manuscript poem will exhibit two voices—one within and one without the boundaries. When we become cognizant of the formidable role allotted to the female poet who must concomitantly have and be, we can grasp the aptness of Dickinson's fascicle poems that reveal the poem that is both itself and not itself, instituting the voices that speak from both within and without the boundaries.

In this extremely formidable role, the woman poet initiates disparate, heteroglossic ways of speaking. Compounded yet further, the position of the woman poet who negotiates motherhood (that is, in the speaking position of motherhood) encounters yet another layer of difficulty. Kristeva "has claimed that it is not *woman* as such who is repressed in patriarchal society, but *motherhood*. The problem remains not women's *jouissance* alone, as Lacan has it in *Encore*, but the necessary relationship between reproduction and *jouissance*" (*Reader* 167). In order to tell themselves, mothers must both be the something and the telling of the something simultaneously—must both be and have. Women cannot inhabit their maternity, Grosz asserts: "In so far as she is mother, woman remains unable to speak her femininity or her maternity" (163).[16] Furthermore, Kristeva appears "to accept that phallic subjects alone, only men, can re-present the unrepresented, subversive underside of the *chora* and the semiotic" (Grosz 164). Problematically, women, it seems, can undergo maternal *jouissance* but not speak of it.

Kristeva's *chora*, a function of the semiotic mode that exists before the symbolic, positions a realm of pulsions and rhythmic drives, a mode precursive to language, and allied with the rhythms of poetry. The semiotic drives distinguish the *chora*, which "precedes and underlies figuration and thus specularization, and is analogous only to vocal or kinetic rhythm" (*Revolution* 26). A space not exactly space, the concept of the *chora* recuperates a mode of motility and energies, of drives that are contradictory, dualistic, and can be represented as the double helix of the DNA or RNA spiral, the dualism rendering "the semiotized body a place of permanent scission" (*Revolution* 27). Kristeva seems to characterize it as existing in the outer reaches, as the other, relative to what exists as dominant; she takes the word *chora* from Plato in *Timeus*, who designates it as receptacle, "unnamable, improbable, hybrid, anterior to naming, to the One, to the father, and consequently, maternally connoted to such an extent that it merits 'not even the rank of a syllable'" (*Desire* 133).

The *chora*, then, a paradox in remaining "unnamable," exists as a mode "anterior to naming." It limns a possibility beyond patriarchal language in that it functions before the name altogether, anterior to the father, and as such "maternally connoted." Aligned with the *chora*, Emily Dickinson's image of the nameless pod is its own sort of unnamable receptacle, its own mode or circumstance anterior to naming. Leon Roudiez, in his introduction to Kristeva, discusses the *chora*, or receptacle, again borrowed from Plato, who describes it as "an invisible and formless being which receives all things and in some mysterious way partakes of the intelligible, and is most incomprehensible" (*Desire* 6).

Partaking of the intelligible and yet remaining incomprehensible: the poem discussed above, "How many Flowers fail in Wood—," identifies with the nameless pod a receptacle of such contradistinctions and possibilities. The four poems purveying the image of a pod occupy places six, eight, ten, and eighteen in the fascicle. Having already broached the tenth, I would like to examine the sixth and eighth before proceeding to explore at further length the eighteenth poem, "My first well Day—since" (Fr288), which describes an event of laying-in of an expecting mother.

The sixth poem of Fascicle Twenty-Eight, "He gave away his Life—" (Fr530), offers a vignette concerning an "obviated bud" that on an ostensible level tracks Christ's effect on his potential followers, at the same time adumbrating the circumstances of gestation. The poem's last lines describe the process by which Christ chooses maturity:

By Blossoms +gradual **process**—
He Chose—Maturity—

And +quickening—as we sowed—
Just obviated Bud—
And when We turned to
note the Growth—
Broke—perfect—from the Pod—
+ Estimate + quick + Common + ripening—[17]

Even a cursory glance at the word variants in the line above displays Dickinson's experimentation with positioning images of pregnancy. In the fascicle the four variants form a line across the bottom of the page: "+ Estimate + quick + Common + ripening—," at least two of which, "quick" and "ripening," apply directly to parturition,[18] so that the workshopping Dickinson we see in this manuscript tips us to her concern with gestation. The presence of the word "quick" as a variant shows, in particular, that Dickinson wished to use a form of that word at least once in the poem.

Meaning "to become alive" in Noah Webster's 1828 *An American Dictionary of the English Language*,[19] the term vectors an important meaning of pregnancy. In her first letter to Thomas Wentworth Higginson, in which she also leans on the word "quick," she presses a connection between poetry and parturition. First she asks Higginson if her "Verse is alive?" and then later in the same letter exhorts him, "Should you think it breathed—and had you the leisure to tell me, I should feel quick gratitude—" (L260). Obviously Dickinson intends the pun on "quick" here, as the entire issue is whether the poetry is "alive." In addition, the dilemma of the woman poet arises in a graphic way when we consider Dickinson's means of signing this letter, demurring when it comes to affixing her signature outright. Dickinson finds naming herself so difficult that she cannot leave her name in the usual place, instead emphasizing the detached nature of naming by trying to reset her speaking position, enclosing her name in a separate envelope. As if out of the play of signification, out of the patriarchal chain, she tries to name herself on her own terms.

The word "quick" enhances the importance of coming to life in the final stanza of "He gave away his Life—," which offers the somewhat riddling, if commonplace, theme that Christ dies so that he can live in his followers. Christ grows within his followers by a gradual or common process, the word variant "Common," proposed as an alternative to "gradual" in the phrase "By Blossoms +gradual **process**—," and the line locates a curious feature of the fascicle in the darkened appearance of the word "process."[20] The organic metaphor of "gradual process" as pregnancy resonates, and likewise holds its resonance if the substitution "+Common" is made. It may be that Dickinson ironizes the word "common" for, though it happens every day, the miraculous event of birth is hardly a mundane process to undergo.[21]

The experience depicted in "He gave away his Life—" hardly fulfills its claims of being gradual, either, for the bud is obviated. When the bud stage of a forming life becomes obviated or eliminated, the process suggests an interrupted pregnancy—a condition opposed to that of being gradual. The obviated bud recalls the "rescinded" (Fr1365) bud of another poem, both of which may indicate an arrested-term pregnancy. The possibility of early termination suggests itself especially through the suggestion of violence in the final line, with the word "broke": "Broke—perfect—from the Pod—."[22] The word "perfect" suggests a status unobtainable by mortal humans born into and living in the world. The line functions somewhat oxymoronically in our understanding of the final action, an ambivalence resting partly on how we weigh the competing phrases "gradual process" with "obviated Bud," and the effect that such weighing has upon the paradoxical word "Broke."

The eighth poem in Fascicle Twenty-Eight, "The Winters are so short—" (Fr532), seems to use the word "pod" as synonymous with house. Of course, houses and their apertures connote the body, as many feminist critics have noted, especially in the Dickinson canon replete with doors and windows and homes. The pod or house in "The Winters are so short—" identifies a specific enclosure that the speaker moves into in the winter, a time when everything else dies:

The Winters are so short—
I'm hardly justified
In sending all the Birds away—
And moving into Pod—

It is important to note that the definition of the word "pod" allows the possibilities both of the legume, which has associations of spring and fruit within, and of the dry container in the fall that holds dormant seeds (and I will discuss below the definition of "pod" according to Dickinson's Webster). Both definitions of "pod" apply here. The pod provides a kind of womb-space in which life can continue while the rest of the world outside remains lifeless, but then, with the changing of seasons, the speaker opens house again when summer returns. This containment vectors the first two and a half stanzas, until in the third stanza the poem hints at crisis, a winter when animals starved and a flood took life away. Wolff asserts that the possibility of annihilation in the deluge "is the deep memory that haunts nature's musings upon the periodic devastation of winter" (353).[23] After the image of the flood, a kind of textual deluge ensues—a page and a half of blank paper following the poem—designating a wash of white in the middle of the fascicle volume.[24]

Finally, the most memorable poem containing a pod, "My first well Day—since" (Fr288), eighteenth in the fascicle, seems to continue the above scenario of lying-in in the winter and opening house in the summer. Having survived a season of illness, the speaker ventures again out into the world:

My first well Day—since
many ill—
I asked to go abroad,
And take the Sunshine in
my hands
And see the things in Pod—

A'blossom just when I went in
To take my + Chance with pain—
Uncertain if myself, or He,
Should prove the + strongest One.

The Summer deepened, while
We strove—
She put Some flowers away—
And Redder cheeked Ones—in
their + stead—
A fond—illusive way—

To cheat Herself, it seemed
she tried—
As if before a child
To + fade—Tomorrow—Rainbows
+ held
The Sepulchre, could hide.

She dealt + a fashion to the
Nut—
She tied the Hoods to Seeds—
She dropped bright scraps
of Tint, about—
And left Brazilian Threads

On every shoulder + that she
met—
Then both her Hands of Haze
Put up—to + hide her
parting Grace
From our + unfitted Eyes—

My loss, by sickness—Was it
Loss?
Or that + Etherial Gain
One Earns by measuring the
Grave—
Then—measuring the Sun—

+ Risk + supplest—lithest—
stoutest + place + die—
+thrust + the + she
could reach + hold + unfur-
nished + seraphic gain,
One gets—

Dickinson almost catalogues *jouissance* here, for the poem burgeons with tropes of fertility: "things in Pod," "A'blossom, "went in," "take my Chance with pain," "Summer deepened," "we strove—," "put some flowers away—," "Redder cheeked Ones—," "before a child," "dealt a fashion to the Nut—," "tied the Hoods to Seeds—." At many cruxes in the poem the undercurrent of gestation becomes stronger than the current of ostensible themes, such as the change of seasons, as for example: "To cheat Herself, it seemed/ she tried—/ As if before a child/ To +fade—Tomorrow—Rainbows/ + held/ The Sepulchre, could hide." One could not find a more resonant euphemism for abortion if one combed through advertisements for cures for menstrual irregularities and regulated courses in mid-nineteenth-century magazines and papers.

The female character may try to cheat herself, as she would cheat herself of a child due to fade tomorrow. The fact that the manuscript page ends with the first line of the fourth stanza adds magnitude to a reading that understands the poem as partially depicting the crisis of the woman attempting to negotiate the consequences of "cheating" herself before a child. "To cheat Herself, it seemed/ she tried—": at this point the reader must turn the fascicle page to continue the phrase and the other part of the analogy. The line's page placement draws attention to the woman's actions in relation to herself, and after the page turn, in relation to the child who may fade tomorrow.

The entire poem depends upon a subtle equation between the opulence of Summer and the problematic gravid condition of the speaker. The period of growth and abundance occurs outside for Summer while the speaker experiences her period of growth inside, in a troubled way. The redder-cheeked flowers that are put away recall the cheeks that are moved away a dimple at a time (Fr567), and also of the flowers that fail in Wood in the earlier fascicle poem. Summer attends actively to the business of giving life, as can be seen in the sexually charged lines that open the fifth stanza. In the last three lines of the fifth stanza, however, she drops scraps and leaves threads, recalling the "moment of Brocade—" and lost "drop—of India" (Fr388), as well as "the little Tint/ That never had a Name—" (Fr567).

The poem recalls Kristeva's injunction that the *chora* may be situated but never posited, because Dickinson lends gestation a topology but without axiomatic form. Its ruptures and rhythms inform the fascicle but defy rhetoric, and in the case of "My first well Day—since," the ruptures almost surpass the rhetoric. The Summer inhabits the surface but the "I" inhabits the rupture so that the poem functions, paradoxically, as a work both gravid and dehiscent. The "I" experiences lying-in while the Summer comes to fruition, "A'blossom"; the fact of two subjects, the "I" and Summer, mimics the problem of experiencing oneself as a dual space. The two continue on parallel paths: the speaker takes her chance with pain, which ends in loss, while the summer deepens. The Summer, likewise, eventually confronts loss, too, near the poem's end when she drops bright scraps, but for at least a while, the Summer flourishes. This is how a woman as mother must signify, how a woman must mother her own duplicitous signification. No wonder Kristeva describes the maternal body as an impossible syllogism:

Cells fuse, split, and proliferate; volumes grow, tissues stretch, and body fluids change rhythm, speeding up or slowing down. Within the body, growing as a graft, indomitable, there is an other. And no one is present within that simultaneously dual and alien space, to signify what is going on. "It happens, but I'm not there." "I cannot realize it, but it goes on." Motherhood's impossible syllogism. (*Desire* 237)

Dickinson maneuvers within this impossible syllogism because she continues to try to find a way of speaking before the signifier. Of course, she must, in a sense, speak patriarchal discourse, but she speaks in a mode before it—that is, the time of *chora*, and herein moves the current and undercurrent of "My first well Day—since." The poem concludes with loss. The "parting Grace" of the Summer must be hidden and the loss of the speaker must be put into perspective, measuring the grave (figuratively, the loss of the unborn child) against the sun. The Summer endorses a parable of the season progressing from spring to fall but it also depicts the loss of the foetus or embryo.[25]

Dickinson enlarges upon summer in another poem, outside Fascicle Twenty-Eight, "Summer—we all have seen—" (Fr1413), in which she depicts an embryo. In this poem, Summer, remote as the moon, is personified, becomes steeped in a confusion of doom, affluence, unknowns, ecstasy, and endowment: "The Doom to be adored—/ Unknown as to an Ecstasy/ The Embryo endowed—." The syntactic elasticity of these lines renders them a quintessential study in signifiers signifying other signifiers, the cross-correspondences webbing the lines with nearly impenetrable linkages.[26] In the poem the narrator believes in and loves the summer, even though she is doomed to lose it; a similar equation exists for the embryo as for summer. The (absent) mother may believe in the embryo as the speaker believes in summer. However one reads these lines, the reader is left missing an omitted part of speech, such as the object of the transitive verb "endowed," who would be the mother, the one who situates the *chora* and who makes this apprehension of ecstasy—and doom—possible.[27] The reading resonates when we see the ecstasy as a kind of gestative *jouissance* without a stated site, and also the doom as a registering of loss, also without a site—both of which are exactly the effect of Dickinson's pod in other poems.

The poetry of Emily Dickinson extends the vision of being able to see the things in pod. If a fundamentally unattainable kind of vision, still it subtends a way to see, a straining toward wanting, a perspective other than the patriarchal. Inevitably the fascicle poem "My first well Day—since" moves from loss to measuring, from pod to poem, *chora* to *différence*; that is, from semiotic to symbolic. Another way of saying this is that inevitably signification closes up over the semiotic because we can only register and understand our experience here in the symbolic. The poem ends in an interrogative that attempts to find discursive meaning in the foregoing loss, signified by "parting Grace." Dickinson launches a monumental, if existential undertaking, though: she

broaches the gap of the semiotic, if only for a second, if only for a pause between signifiers, to glimpse the thing in pod, before language ushers the poem
back into the symbolic.

Cogently enough, the movement from pod to poem mentioned above
might be traced, literally, in Dickinson's lexicon, from the word "pod" to the
word "poem," in Noah Webster's 1828 dictionary, in which the word "pod"
precedes the word "poem." Famous for referring to and living by her lexicon,
Dickinson might have found Noah Webster's definition of "pod" appealing.
First of all, the word is a little mysterious for its sourcelessness: "[In W. *podi* signifies to take in or comprehend; but I know not from what source we have this
word.]" Webster proceeds to discuss the usage of the word, and the distinction
between pods that are siliques and the pods that are spoken of as legumes, concluding that in New England the word is used in the latter sense. Immediately
following, Webster then designates the verb form "pod," meaning, importantly, "To swell; to fill; also to produce pods." Following the entry "pod," in
direct order, are the words "podagric," "podded," "podder" (the last two both
versions of "pod"), "podge" ("a puddle; a plash"), and then "poem." The definition of "poem" derives from the Greek, "to make, to compose songs." Webster
adds, of the Russian variation, "to sing," that the "radical sense is the same, to
strain." Thus the poet "strains," and in the case of Fascicle Twenty-Eight, perhaps, "swells" and "fills" as in the definition of "pod," too. (In Chapter 6 I will
detail further feminine associations for the pod, according to Dickinson's biology text classifications). Perhaps it is not simply coincidence that the words
"poet" and "pod" carry similar vowel and consonant sounds.

The concerns with "measuring the/ Grave," at the end of "My first well
Day—since" are addressed again in a subsequent poem, "Unit, like Death, for
Whom?" (F543). As a poem that presents "the Bearer—/ and the Borne—," it
suggests parturitive significance:

Unit, like Death, for Whom?
True, like the Tomb,
Who tells no secret
Told to Him—
The Grave is strict—
Tickets admit
Just two—the Bearer—
and the Borne—
And seat—just One—
The Living—tell—
The Dying—but a syllable—
The Coy Dead—None—
No Chatter—here—no tea—

So Babbler, and Bohea—stay there—
But Gravity—and Expectation—and
Fear—
A tremor just, that All's not sure.

In this poem pregnancy forms an understated issue. Only two have gained tickets for admission—the bearer and the borne[28]—and the mention of "Gravity—and Expectation—" in the prepenultimate line also connote gestation. While Dickinson's 1828 Webster makes no mention of connotations of pregnancy in the word "expectation" or its forms, it does do so with the word "gravity." "Gravity" derives from a Latin root, *gravis*, which means heavy, and that root word is listed under both the word "gravity" and "gravid," which means "Pregnant; being with child." Moreover, after "*gravis*, heavy," Webster notes, "See *Grave*." Hence, the use of the word "gravity" here imbricates notions of both death and pregnancy, a perfectly knotted word in a poem of possible aggravated childbirth.

Moreover, "Unit, like Death, for Whom?" preoccupies itself with the nature of telling as it descries the possibilities of signification at the brink. There is "No Chatter—here—no tea—," a fascinating line that avers the lack of talk for the dead. The living tell easily; in fact, they chatter. But the dying, those on the brink, tell "but a syllable."[29] Dickinson displays herein the disintegration of language at the boundary of death.

The prepenultimate line commands those who talk to "stay there—." Hence, the lines of division begin to form; yet if she enjoins the babblers to stay on one side—"there"—who then is on the side of "here"? Significantly, the "here" provides the side for the ones who don't talk, the ones who are gravid. This command would seem to situate the readers on the talking side, while it positions the poet, oddly, on the side of silence. Perhaps the command to "stay there—" forms a directive that only a woman poet would give—and especially a woman poet operating from the speaking-position of gestation. She thus places herself on the side of uncertainty, commanding the talkers to "stay there—" perhaps as a subtle rejoinder to the question "for Whom?" of the first line. Given the interrogative "Unit, like Death, for Whom?," the answer may indicate that death aligns itself as a unit with the speaker, who is, oddly, on the other side from babbling or talking at all.

The final line, in fact, recuperates the pulsions of the semiotic in its evocative phrase, "A tremor just": one single tremor, a physical sensation, returns the poem to the basic drives characterizing the *chora*. In this poem, Dickinson may give us both the brink before birth of "the Borne" and the brink before death of "the Dying." That Dickinson can push her thinking to the furthest reaches of those brinks of life and death becomes clear in other poems: "Love—is anterior to Life—/ Posterior—to Death—" (Fr980), she states, in an outrageous stretching of ontological boundaries; again, she posits that "Love—is that later Thing than Death—/ More previous—than Life—" (Fr840). That she can push gestation to a site previous to life and oppose it to a site later than death alerts us to her consuming need to push signification past all boundaries. She works a dangerous business, extending language in that way, eschewing certainty, inviting annihilation. And no wonder "Unit, like Death, for Whom?" resolves in antiresolution and disjunction: "A tremor just, that All's not sure."

She does not make the comparatively offhand claim, however, that nothing is sure; the phrasing is more embracing, more adamant, more nihilistic, starting with "all": "*All's* not sure" (emphasis added). The Unit, whatever and for whomever it is, has gone the progress of a single item to an "all" in the conclusion. The discrete measurement of one has become the indeterminate, slippery "all"—an all that's finally precarious. Despite the trembling syllable, and despite the informality of the contraction used in the line, which might seem to claim caution, she makes in this *dénouement* a large statement of uncertainty.

Fascicle Twenty-Eight begins and ends with the uncertainty of language, as the poet considers the relationship of signifier to signified, which forms a major current of the fascicle;[30] an undercurrent, however, is formed by the web of associations created by the images of the pod. Probably the poet needs both current and undercurrent, and these together locate her duplicity. As some feminist critics have asserted, the quintessential problem for women writers arises from the dilemma of being positioned within language that depends upon the phallus as its structuring term. The predicament can be phrased as follows:

If woman is nothing but a category within language, constructed by male desire, where and what are women? If language structures sexuality around the male term, is there no female sexuality that is other? Can women be retrieved from the dominance of the phallic term? If women are beyond the phallus, where are they? (Garner, Kahane, Sprengnether 22)

By forming an undercurrent of parturition, Dickinson may be finding a way for one woman, who seeks an alternative to the Name-of-the-Father, to speak.

Instances of the "pod" image continue to resonate when Dickinson uses the word "cocoon" in the first poem of the next fascicle, "From Cocoon forth a Butterfly" (Fr610). This continuance of the pod in a parallel image testifies to the value of reading Dickinson's poems in fascicle form, as we see new indices of associations. It hardly seems coincidental that the first poem of Fascicle Twenty-Seven contains the word "pod," and that the first poem of Fascicle

Twenty-Nine begins with a kind of similar image, "cocoon," so that the four instances of "pod" in the middle fascicle become consolidated.

Recognizing the concentration of poems using the term "pod" in Fascicle Twenty-Eight allows us to see outside the fascicle to its neighboring fascicles, and also to unpacketed poems. For instance, another poem written most likely later than the poems in fascicles Twenty-Seven, Twenty-Eight, and Twenty-Nine refers to a pod in an intriguing if distant way:

The joy that has no stem nor core,
Nor seed that we can sow,
Is edible to longing,
But ablative to show.

By fundamental palates
Those products are preferred
Impregnable to transit
And patented by pod. (Fr1762)

The terms of procreation run throughout the brief poem: core, seed, sow, impregnable, pod. Moreover, the reference to ablation—the removal of a growth—informs the fourth line. If the poem considers the issue of abortion then the "products," if afforded a somewhat literalist reading, may refer to the readily procured medicines and procedures for abortion that were available in Dickinson's time:

Many women continued in the decades after 1840 to bring about abortion in their homes through use of the pills, fluid extracts, and medicinal oils that were nonpublicly marketed with such suggestive names as the "Female Regulator," "Periodical Drops," "Uterine regulator," and "Woman's Friend." Ely Van de Warker, a Syracuse, New York, gynecologist who studied American abortion methods, noted that "every schoolgirl knows the meaning of these terms." (Brodie 225)

In any case, the usage of the signifier "pod" returns in later Dickinson writings, though in this instance it seems less intimate than in the poems of Fascicle Twenty-Eight.

If perhaps anachronistic to cast Emily Dickinson's Fascicle Twenty-Eight strictly in the terms of twentieth-century theory, still it is worthwhile to consider the dilemma faced by nineteenth-century women writers in a light that shows clearly the difficulties they faced. Dickinson displays in her poetry the prolepsis inherent in the work of a nineteenth-century woman writer attempting to find her speaking voice, especially as she had to have experienced frustration in facing the phallic term, and uncertainty in deciding what paradigm might be causing such restraint upon the process of signification. Fascicle

Twenty-Eight generates a workshop for that dilemma, allowing the image of the pod to operate as a kind of *chora* in the 1800s—but a *chora* endangered. Dickinson, of all poets, discovered a way to adjust the phallic term, pushing language to its limits, not only on the side of death and after death, but also on the side of birth and before birth.

The poem with which this chapter commenced, "How many Flowers fail in Wood—," states the dilemma most succinctly: "How many Cast a nameless Pod/ Opon the nearest Breeze—/ Unconscious of the Scarlet Freight—/ It bear to Other Eyes—." What is "nameless" is without the ability to be made conscious in the patriarchal workings of language, so that the pod image reconfigures the circumstance of women writing from a position of nameless-ness in a phallic culture. Dickinson out-others the other in this poem, aligning the namelessness of women by means of suggesting the *chora*. Lacanian theory iterates that we utilize the Name-of-the-Father, the phallus as signifier, in order to enter the symbolic order—and to the extent that we do, the struggle posed by that paradox becomes the first order of business for any woman poet. Dickinson descries a project of recursion, trying, as Nicodemus did, to reenter the womb with language and to come back still speaking.[31] If there were ever any alternative to the Name-of-the-Father, then Dickinson broaches that boundary; if there were ever any female naming alongside the signifier, then Dickinson supplies it.

CHAPTER 4

Word, Birth, and Poe's Alchemy

In the foregoing chapters I have traced each poet's use of gestation, detailing its relation to signification. Poe and Whitman incur upon maternal space, and Dickinson, in her suggestion of abbreviated pregnancy, portrays a difficult, interrupted gestative process. Poe's goal remains entry into the site of language; Whitman's the transgression of the female realm in order to effect the cooptation of feminine *jouissance*; Dickinson's the encoding of scission that, troubled as it is, depicts egress from the symbolic mode. In "The Raven," Poe shows in his "Nevermore" a way to capture the moment of desire for language as he attempts to replace the desire for the mother. Whitman's "omnific semiotics" characterize him as a "mother man" in "Song of Myself," eager to accrue the benefits of *chora* as a new means by which he might utter himself. In Fascicle Twenty-Eight, Dickinson educes miscarrying circumstances that, cogently for the problematic position of woman as speaker who must try to enter symbolic discourse, provide a glimpse of one way a nineteenth-century woman poet learns to speak in patriarchal culture.

The next three chapters examine cultural influences on the usage of language for each poet. The influences I explore are highly specific—alchemy, hydropathy, and botany, as they existed in nineteenth-century ideology and as they concern, respectively, Poe, Whitman, and Dickinson. Each cultural influence can be seen at least in part as a metaphor for birth: alchemy offers the terms of regeneration, hydropathy depends oftentimes upon creating a liquid generative space, and botany presents graphic representations of the procreative process. The three poets concern themselves, respectively, with signification as a process of regeneration, liquidity, and botanical process. These cultural influences, in addition, also afford applications to language. In the naming described in these chapters, the poets each discover a cultural corollary that serves to corroborate and exemplify a matrilineal type of naming that interrogates more conventional ways of naming.

Poe's matrilineal naming occurs in his ranging among female names. Especially in his later poems, many of which carry female cognomens, the speaker witnesses repeatedly the death and resuscitation of women subjects. Women's names generate and regenerate throughout his corpus, in a flurry of life and death peculiar to Edgar Allan Poe, and the influence of alchemy can be associated with such a movement among names. Poe clearly was enamored of alchemical processes, as Randall Clack argues persuasively in his *The Marriage of Heaven and Earth*, in which he claims that "the tropes and metaphors of alchemy provided Taylor, Poe, Hawthorne, and Fuller with not only a variation of the transformation theme but also a temporal link in their metaphors with the unknown," pointing out that alchemy offered "a unique way of imagining the transformation/regeneration process" (9). The esoteric process of transmuting nothing into something, of bringing life from that which is dead, describes an early science that could hardly have proved less than fascinating to the Poe concerned with the birth site of language.

In fact, the magical-scientific ability to wrest life from next to nothing could come close to standing in as a kind of *ars poetica* for his work. Poe, whose famous assertion that the most poetical topic is the death of a beautiful woman, has been somewhat misperceived in his poems and stories because of that assertion. In "The Philosophy of Composition," Poe avers that "the death, then, of a beautiful woman is, unquestionably, the most poetical topic in the world—and equally is it beyond doubt that the lips best suited for such a topic are those of a bereaved lover" (*Essays* 19). While he may have claimed a beautiful woman's death as aesthetic, what he actually captures most memorably in both fiction and poetry is the dying and *resurrecting* and dying of a beautiful woman. The indeterminacy of the ending of "Ligeia," for example, follows this pattern, as does that of "The Fall of the House of Usher." The longevity of those two stories can be adduced to Ligeia's and Madeline's *refusal* to die, and the stories' inability fully to rescusitate each. The same holds for the poetry, in a large body of Poe's most gripping poems: the beautiful woman dies and revives, *ad infinitum* in a way we might almost describe as the alchemical transformation/regeneration process.

Edgar Allan Poe, well versed in studies of alchemy, read carefully such works as Isaac D'israeli's 1823 *Curiosities of Literature* and William Godwin's 1834 *Lives of the Necromancers*. Kevin Hayes contends that Poe reviewed Godwin's *Lives of the Necromancers* and knew D'israeli well: "He [Poe] referred to Disraeli multiple times and plundered his works to fill the odd corners of magazines he edited" (100). Clack, too, mentions these sources, and others as well, as for instance Winthrop's collection: "Poe would have also found a virtual treasure trove consisting of hundreds of alchemical books and pamphlets that once belonged to John Winthrop, Jr., at the New York Hospital and the New York Society Library" (45).

William Godwin's *Lives of the Necromancers* introduces a section on "alchymy" as follows: "To make our catalogue of supernatural doings, and the lawless imaginations of man, the more complete, it may be necessary to refer to the craft, so eagerly cultivated in successive ages of the world, of converting the inferior metals into gold, to which was usually joined the *elixir vitae*, or universal medicine, having the quality of renewing the youth of man, and causing him to live for ever" (43). Godwin's introduction of the craft of alchemy includes the most essential elements—that is, the transmutation of metals and the renewal of life. Both transmutation and renewal constitute properties embraced in Poe's poetry, his lyricism evidencing those seemingly magical changes throughout. Godwin emphasizes that alchemy existed for centuries, the first authentication of it provided by an edict of Diocletian, around 300 BC, who demanded that all alchemical books (addressing the making of gold and silver) in Egypt be destroyed; alchemy, however, almost certainly existed prior to Diocletian, with records of Solomon, Pythagoras, and Hermes as practitioners (Godwin 43). Throughout antiquity, it was renewal and regeneration that composed the sought-for result of alchemists' machinations.

Isaac D'israeli, as well, in *Curiosities of Literature* stresses renewal through alchemy. When describing the works of ancient alchemists, he states that "we find authentic accounts of some who have lived three centuries, with tolerable complexions, possessed of nothing but a crucible and a bellows! but they were so unnecessarily mysterious, that whenever such a person was discovered, he was sure in an instant to disappear, and was never afterwards heard of" (87). We might be relieved that those who lived for three centuries would be blessed with "tolerable complexions," and lament that they proved so "unnecessarily mysterious"; in any case such tongue-in-cheek humor characterizes the accounts given in *Curiosities of Literature*, but most importantly D'israeli, like Godwin, emphasizes regeneration and transmutation.

For instance, he notes Van Helmont's attempts at regeneration: "Van Helmont, who could not succeed in discovering the true elixir of life, however hit on the spirit of hartshorn, which for a good while he considered was the wonderful elixir itself, restoring to life persons who seemed to have lost it" (87). Again giving an account laced with humor, he recounts Van Helmont's seeming discovery of the elixir: "And though this delightful enthusiast could not raise a ghost, yet he thought he had; for he raised something aerial from spa-water, which mistaking for a ghost, he gave it that very name; a name which we still retain in *gas*, from the German *geist*, or ghost!" (87). Another alchemist, Paracelsus, kept these tiny spirits handy in his sword hilt, and evidenced, too, an obsession with transmutation, describing in a recipe "the impurity which is to be transmuted into such purity" (88). Paracelsus's recipe was for the creation of a fairy out of dung, but such was the delicacy of the scientist that once "having furnished a recipe to make a fairy, [he] had the delicacy to refrain from its formation" (90).

Transmutation here, as so often in fiction depicting the alchemist or mad scientist, encodes the desire to coopt the functions of female reproduction, as with the most obvious example of Mary Shelley's *Frankenstein*. In the largest sense, alchemy is concerned with the "desire to penetrate the mystery of life," wanting to change that which is not human so it can be "intensified and raised to a nobler form than that" from which it derives (Read 2). As such, transmutation and regeneration encrypt male transgression of female parturition.

Poe depends upon such presumption of regenerative powers. Clack recognizes alchemical transmutation in several Poe tales, including the hoaxes "Von Kempelen and His Discovery," "The Colloquy of Monos and Unas," and "The Assignation," among others. In "The Assignation," because the alchemist acts prominently to restore life in a kind of rebirth, Poe suggests the cooptation of reproduction. A hoax, the story depends for its plot upon the death and rebirth of a child. "The Assignation" begins with a description of a drowning child, and continues with descriptions of the actions of others attempting to rescue the child, during which a figure sits in the shadows, seemingly unconcerned, and strums a guitar. The figure is the father of the child, who ultimately, because of the ability of music to construct purity from impurity, saves the child. English alchemist Robert Fludd, a name Poe cites in Roderick Usher's library, believed that the relationship between music and alchemy represented "'an ascent from imperfection to perfection, from impurity to purity'" (Ammann cited in Clack 52). What is striking about the story is the prevailing power of the father over the mother, who through his seeming inaction, or at least his confounding lack of engagement in the usual methods of rescue, is able to secure regeneration when no one else can. The boy is reborn from the water.

Poe introduces alchemy in his poetry, too, explicitly in the poem "Introduction." The poem contains many of the principles of alchemy, perhaps by chance or perhaps by design. For example, blackness (mentioned twice in lines 16–17) comprises a characteristic of the laboratories and smudged skin of alchemists, and hence is associated with the study generally. In addition, the poem mixes music with alchemy, a common admixture, as seen above. Interestingly, Poe uses alchemy as a trope for the experience of reading poetry when he was a little boy:

For, being an idle boy lang syne,
Who read Anacreon, and drank wine,
I early found Anacreon rhymes
Were almost passionate sometimes—
And by strange alchemy of brain
His pleasures always turn'd to pain—
His naivete to wild desire—
His wit to love—his wine to fire—(157)

By the "strange alchemy of brain," oddly, Poe's alchemy turns pleasure into pain. Poetry seems to render the world mutable; after reading passionate poetry, in the series of transformations immediately following the mention of alchemy, a kind of transmutation of emotional and other states occurs, in which naivete changes to desire, wit becomes love, wine becomes fire. The usage of the trope of alchemy allows Poe to depict his unstable world, a cosmology of volatile elements ready to transform into other states. Since the poem operates as a kind of *Bildungsdichte*, detailing the development of the boy into a man of passion and dreams and art, the prominence of alchemy as the image of poetic transformation should not be underread.

Others of Poe's poems offer similar evocations of the ancient lore of alchemy, as in the poem "Stanzas," which describes a person who seems to come to birth from the elements: "Whose fervid, flick'ring torch of life was lit/ From the sun and stars . . ." (77). Moreover, "Stanzas" invokes "ancient lore," exactly the same point from which "The Raven" is launched: "Once upon a midnight dreary, while I pondered, weak and weary,/ Over many a quaint and curious volume of forgotten lore—" (364). If we wonder what volumes of ancient lore the speaker of "The Raven" ponders, setting his reverie in motion, we might remember that if his library is anything like Roderick Usher's, it contains authors like Robert Fludd, mentioned above, an alchemist whose Fluddean philosophy is based upon a "mystical chemical account of the Creation" (Debus 17). It is hardly unreasonable to imagine that the volumes of ancient lore that spark the imagination of the speaker of "The Raven" include those volumes of alchemy famous for their vivid and sometimes lurid illustrations, and that they affect the speaker in the strange way that the brain of the boy in the poem "Introduction" was affected. Sitting by the fireplace, in the presence of each "dying ember [which] wrought its ghost upon the floor" (365), the speaker delivers perhaps the entire poem of "The Raven" as the result of a night's reading in the forgotten alchemical lore.

Finally, the poem "Eldorado" hinges upon a knowledge of alchemy. Mabbott pronounces "Eldorado" as "the noblest of Poe's poems, the most universal in implication, and the most intensely personal" (461), and credits it with a subtlety of message. "Eldorado" depends upon Poe's reading of D'israeli's *Curiosities of Literature* (Poe, *Collected Works* 462), as well as upon the historical event of the California Gold Rush of 1849. The lure of easy gold coaxing thousands to a difficult or even fatal move west was an event of which Poe was well aware. Significantly, the lure of easy gold lies at the heart of alchemical quests, too, as Godwin notes when he states of alchemy that "the object [was] unbounded wealth" (44). The connection between the gold rush and alchemy is far from transitory or accidental in the work of Poe, because both the poem "Eldorado" and the story "Von Kempelen and His Discovery" resulted from his interest in the Gold Rush (Poe, *Collected Works* 461–62). In the story, Von Kempelen maintains a laboratory in a garret closet, filled with furnace, crucibles, a tube, lead, and the dissipation of a vaporous liquid. Von Kempelen seeks through his experiments to discover the philosopher's stone, "an ill-defined something" (Redgrove 1), the ultimate hoped-for realization of alchemists, the means by which regeneration might be effected. The philosopher's stone allowed transmutation, and because of the "alchemical doctrine of the unity of all things," alchemists believed that "all bodies possess a common basis in the *prima materia*, or single primordial matter" found in the philosopher's stone (Read 120).

In the story, Von Kempelen seeks the philosopher's stone in order to make alchemical gold, and in the poem "Eldorado," the knight seeks Eldorado, the land of gold. Both quest after chimeras, gold that cannot be possessed, and both are visionaries in their own ways. Mabbott points out that "by Poe's day 'Eldorado' had come to mean a place, the object of search, where gold (or good fortune) was to be found" (464). The knight begins well-dressed—happy and riding in the sunshine—but ends as a shadow who is failing, continuing his hopeless quest, and riding in the light of the moon. The poem details this failure:

> But he grew old—
> This knight so bold—
> And o'er his heart a shadow
> Fell, as he found
> No spot of ground
> That looked like Eldorado. (463)

The gold he seeks is as elusive as the gold the alchemist seeks. The alchemist attempts to make a valuable metal out of lead, a metal of little worth, and the seeker of Eldorado, the gold rush pioneer, similarly attempts to find a valuable metal from next to nothing. Both are doomed to failure, the first experiencing a loss of vision, the second a loss of resources and perhaps health and life. The failure of vision comprises a theme, from "Tamerlane" forth, and including the speaker with the strange alchemy of brain in "Introduction," to which Poe returns many times, and many times embellishes.

Alchemy operates as a means for Poe to involve himself in language and expression. To the extent that language forms a relationship with his audience, the image of alchemy affords a way for Poe to shake his readers from their preconceived notions about the world. "In the philosophy of the medieval alchemists," states Clack, "Poe found a ready-made system of tropes and allegories that offered as its ultimate goal not merely the creation of the mythical philosophers' stone and the transmutation of base metal into gold, but intimations of a process that might transmute (through the power of imagination) his readers' mundane perceptions of the material world into visionary experiences of the supernal realm" (51). Even more than a way to shake his readers, though, the ancient lore of the alchemists provided Poe with a way to further his absolute devotion to the power of the word.

Alchemical texts reveal themselves indirectly, famous for their sometimes exasperatingly cryptic expression. Gareth Roberts states that "alchemists' love of metaphor, enigma, allegory and riddle often means that the normal modes of alchemical discourse are figurative not literal" (8). Alchemists use pervasive techniques of what seems like obfuscation to some and illumination to others, and it is sometimes hard to tell the difference, as Roberts asserts: "it is not always clear whether the allegories occupying some or all of alchemical treatises are figurative expressions concealing practical processes from the vulgar, and revealing them through a veil to the initiate, or whether the medium is the message and the allegory is meant to reveal some other meaning" (66). This enigmatical feature of the expression of the alchemists would have been one that Poe, the writer of hoaxes and riddles and puzzles, most certainly found attractive and instructive; master of the abstruse, Poe borrowed liberally from such techniques. As Burland sees it, "the spirit of poetic symbolism is also a root of alchemical methods of expression" (7). Moreover, the most serious alchemist used such language to track the "discovery of his own soul," a path described by C. G. Jung in the twentieth century, when he found that images from alchemy "were reflected in the dreams and daydreams" of some of his patients (Burland 139). Alchemy, thus, presents itself in all its evocative diction as a pervading allegory for the individual's search for identity, one that Poe draws upon in his

Bildungsdichte "Introduction" chronicling the strange alchemy of brain involved in the reading of poetry.

Poe borrows from alchemy primarily in the incorporation of images of transmutation and regeneration, and in the writing of poems of women's names, which comprise a major part of his corpus. Specifically, he uses the principles of transmutation and regeneration to show his heroine flickering between life and death; what the transmutation of Ligeia/Rowena accomplishes, the body of later poems also accomplishes, though in flashcard style—that is, flicking through the poems moving from existence to extinction. D'israeli addresses regeneration when he exclaims that, "never was a philosophical imagination more beautiful than that exquisite *Paligenesis*, as it has been termed from the Greek, or a regeneration" (89). He describes the process of regeneration, the "picture of immortality," as follows: "The semina of resurrection are concealed in extinct bodies, as in the blood of man; the ashes of roses will again revive into roses, though smaller and paler than if they had been planted; unsubstantial and unodoriferous, they are not roses which grow on rose-trees, but their delicate apparitions; and, like apparitions, they are seen but for a moment!" (89). Famous for such transmutation in his fiction, Poe creates most notably with the figure of Ligeia/Rowena, a corpse at half-life who teeters in the middle of the room at the end of the short story "Ligeia." Through such death and rebirth of characters, we see "Poe's literary adaptation of alchemical death and resurrection (*solve et coagula*)," and "indeed, Rowena is transmuted into Ligeia" (Clack 58). As Poe works from Ligeia to Rowena to Ligeia in his story, so does he work from Lenore to Eulalie to Ulalume in his poems.

In "The Fall of the House of Usher," Madeline, too, undergoes regeneration and a kind of resurrection, her tomb recalling "the chemical death in an alchemist's alembic" (Clack 59). Even more, however, her long lying-in between the states of death and life, and her final walk, still on the cusp between death and life, lend the ultimate suspense to the story, and what seems to be the real heart of Poe's philosophical and emotional concern—the real obsession, I suppose, of his art. Transmutation prevails, as the poet remains fascinated by the state of not-quite-life and not-quite-death.

Poe's ranging among the proper names of women, one of the most noticeable characteristics in his poetry, is also one of the most necessary survival tactics he uses as a writer wielding the signifier. With the shifting among female names Poe trips down lines of seemingly female-defined devolutions. I describe Poe's technique, allied with the concatenation of female names, as "lying," by which he incorporates at the same time dying and reviving, and allies his poetry with the powers of transmutation. The poems devolve woman to woman, notably by first name rather than surname, even though the women prove to be neither alive nor dead, neither body nor name altogether, but names lying on the brink because they signify both what is and what isn't.

Poe progresses from woman's name to woman's name, Annie to Helen to Annabel Lee, and as he ranges he describes an uneasy shuffling among proper names. The shuffling turns his speaking position more and more ghostly, as the speaker becomes entangled within the names of female beloveds. In the poems of women's names—and such poems prove manifold in Poe's poetic canon—the critical insight that Poe's work demonstrates "displacement as names name other names" (Williams 7) shows perspicaciously. This matrilineal shuffling clearly doesn't work in the orderly way of a family history in which a patronymic devolves generation to generation; instead each woman's name replaces each of the others within the chain of signification, and they seem to occur almost randomly in his oeuvre, regenerating poem to poem.[1] Poe's women's names exemplify the *glissement* of movement, signifier to signifier, as they exhibit the concept that the only signified for a signifier is another signifier—that we're caught in the loop.

The women of Poe's poetry should always die if we take seriously Poe's notorious dictum, stated above, that art's proper subject is the death of a beautiful woman. The women in his poetry, however, *seem* to die, which is another matter, or sometimes die and then come back to life. Apparently, what *ars* might have dictated to Poe, practice confounded, for the women are always becoming almost deceased. In his poetry, Poe creates the afore mentioned Ligeias and Madelines who become regenerated, as he does for example in the poem "Lenore," in which he presents the title character with "The life upon her yellow hair, but not within her eyes—."[2] In case the effect might become lost on the reader, he repeats the paradox in the line immediately following: "The life still there upon her hair, the death upon her eyes."[3] By desiring a lover who may or may not be dead, Poe raises some unusual questions about desire and the nature of language: for instance, if desire gives rise to language, then what place does the desire that is necrophilia have in relation to language? Furthermore, what might be the relation of decomposition to composition? Does he, in desiring a lover who is alive/dead, attempt to reach the cusp between signifier and signified?

As a reader of Poe, Jacques Lacan suggests that the signifier orients the subject in Poe's "The Purloined Letter," and he draws on Freud to show that "it is the symbolic order which is constitutive for the subject" ("Seminar" 40). In other words, C. Auguste Dupin arrives at his relation to the story's mystery by assessing his relationship with the signifiers, which involve the purloined letters of language. The impetus of the story derives from "the decisive orientation which the subject receives from the itinerary of a signifier" ("Seminar" 40). Barbara Johnson remarks that "the letter does not function as a unit of meaning (a signified) but as that which produces certain effects (a signifier)" (115), and just as the purloined letter acts as the signifier that is constitutive for the subject, so the sliding signification of desired women's names determines the relationalities for the speaker of Poe's poems of women.

No sooner does Poe's speaker love than he witnesses the demise of the beloved, only to repeat the pattern in another poem with another woman, who is also part corpse, part woman. Poe represents his women by moving *ad nauseam* from signifier to signifier: Helen to Lenore to Annabel Lee to Eulalie to Adeline to Annie to Ulalume. Even Poe himself, to some extent, seems to have been aware of the interchangeability of women's names; on the copy of the poem "Lenore" that he gave to Sarah Helen Whitman, he wrote, "Helen, Ellen, Elenore, Lenore" (Mabbott 331).[4] The proper names nearly interchangeable, the signifiers proliferate seemingly in accord with only one signified; that is to say, each woman's name correlates with the same odd signified, a half-dead, half-alive woman, or more precisely, slides signifier to signifier, one name signifying the next.[5] As Jonathan Elmer notices of "Lenore," "there is no 'fact' of Lenore, dead or alive, that is not a fact of language" (213). In other words, the women of Poe's poems exist not as women, but as language, as names that are neither living nor dead.

The poet's job remains that of recognizing his speaker's subject position in the midst of these signifiers. Lacan suggests that the threshold of language corresponds to the threshhold of the subconscious, especially as represented by Freudian dream theory; hence, for Lacan, the process of displacement in dreams (one idea moves from image to image) functions as the process of metonymy in language. Poe metonymizes in the women of his poems the speaker's relationship with one idea, and that one idea is that decomposition exists. Poe's type of composition descries the frenetic activity of making before the subject itself is unmade; his writing unravels in the process.[6]

"Ulalume," for instance, comprises a poem about a name more than about a person of that name; the name "Ulalume" identifies just one of the interchangeable names.[7] The narrator and Psyche take a gloomy October walk, only to find at the end of their journey the name of Ulalume:

And I said—"What is written, sweet sister,
On the door of this legended tomb?"
She replied—"Ulalume—Ulalume!—
'T is the vault of thy lost Ulalume!" (418)

Poe at the same time kills and revives Ulalume, for on the tomb the name is "legended"—that is, both mythical and written. The name of this beloved remains alive forever in her fame exactly because of the record of her as a name on the stone of her grave. In this way Poe en-graves his signifiers of women. The defiles of the signifier, for this nineteenth-century poet, become the instruments of ultimate acts of composition and decomposition. The legended signifier identifies the poet's generativity at the same time that it encompasses his recognition of death. Just as the speaker discovers signification his heart grows "ashen and sober" as the "sere" leaves—the leaves of October as well as the leaves of his text.

No sooner does he signify his beloved than he begins to change her from life to written life, so that what he has left is the page. Though he claims twice in the final four lines of the penultimate stanza that he can "know, now" who tempted him to arrive at this occasion, he will not say. The answer, of course, is "Ulalume"—not the woman, but the signifier. "Ulalume" provides the name he has searched for, and his quest has been not for the woman but for the word; that is to say, that which can be "legended" has led him to the site of en-graving. Poe seeks throughout his poems "the secret that lies in these wolds" (418), a secret kept until the speaker arrives at the tomb and reads.

Reading the legended signifier unlocks "the thing that lies hidden in these wolds" (418)—namely, the word, and Poe concentrates on the word that is specifically a proper name. Poe constructs one-signifier discourses; in the end, it's all that he knows, with absolute authority, how to say. The Poe speaker, who experienced difficulty in saying the "Nevermore" in "The Raven," attempts to dredge meaning by displacing one signifier with another in the poems of women's names. Hence, the obsessively repeated "Annabel Lee," in the poem by that name, demonstrates another metonymic shuffling of the female eponym.

The first utterance of the name in the poem "Annabel Lee" clarifies the fact that we again confront signifier as much as persona, as Poe designates in the fourth line: "By the name of Annabel Lee" (477). She exists as one both dead and alive, both consigned to sepulchre and fixing the narrator with her "bright eyes." In this poem Poe so consummates the desire for the female body (that is really the name) that he depicts the narrator managing to "lie down by the side" of his "darling" signifier.[8] The action of lying proves a significant one in the Poe-esque arena of shuffling referents, for his lying down forms an act of sexual advance at the same time that it indicates his own lying down to death. His action as a speaking subject replicates the action of his strange signifiers that come into creation even as they erase themselves, then transmute to other signifiers, in seemingly endless regeneration. Annabel Lee is the epitome of a good "lie."[9]

She also offers with her name the only utterance Poe can give, because her name is the only way he can say, given that his saying exemplifies skilled prevarication. "Annabel Lee" designates a term that indicates at once what is and what is not, that refers to a woman both alive and dead: the signifier heralds its own absence. Jefferson Humphries notes more generally that for Poe, "the moment of possession and totalization, is, like the purloined letter, like the raven, like the grotesque in general, a pure signifier" (61). When Poe's narrator wants to "lie down by the side" of Annabel Lee, Poe gives the lie to all that is legended, and what is legended decomposes even as it is composed. While the narrator has come a little further than the narrator of "The Raven," he has come not much further; in "Annabel Lee" the final word is not in the narrator's but in the voice of the "sounding sea."

The act of lying, for Poe, suggests death and sex as well as voice that utters the infinitely flickering signifier. In creating the speaker who lies, Poe creates he who can authorize his own relationship with intersubjectivity. With the use of lying the poet tries to eject the silence, though the coming to voice may prove limited, often limited to the one signifier. The signifier operates in a particular way, undoing itself, and this forms the process I call decomposition.[10] Poe's power of articulation tends toward the metonymic, in that his articulation doesn't proceed and continue; rather, it finds its one term only to discover the danger of its erasure, and then replaces the term with another signifier of equal value that in turn begins its erasure, and so on: Helen becomes Ulalume becomes Lenore, and so on.

Important to my notion of Poe's decomposition, the Poe-esque signifier corresponds simultaneously to what does and does not exist and, more exactly, corresponds to that which is in the act of becoming undone—"undone" in the realms of both signification and nineteenth-century connotations of female sexuality. The signifier, to begin with, symbolizes absence: "the signifier is a unit in its very uniqueness, being by nature symbol only of an absence" (Lacan, "Seminar" 54). In "The Raven" Poe's speaker attempts to take on the signifier "Nevermore" in order to represent his experience of the mother's absence. Poe's intersubjectivity as evinced in his female signifier both is and is not and oscillates between being and nonbeing even as Poe's speaker speaks.[11] Toward this condition, specifically, Poe discovers dissembling as poetic strategy; furthermore, because the signifier represents what will both be and not be, lying uncovers the speaker's location with regard to signification in the most cogent, forthright way possible—by acknowledging that it both is and isn't. The lie locates a condition by which a thing exists not in the material world, but in language only.

As one of the most crucial aspects of Poe's poetic program, lying vectors his conception of sex with his overriding theme of the fear of death. By loving she whose ontological status is uncertain he integrates a strategy for making language as it unmakes reality—an accomplished discourse of lying. In "Romance" (which repeats the opening lines of "Introduction"), the narrator creates the primal scene of utterance, in which he says a bird

Taught me my alphabet to say—
To lisp my very earliest word
While in the wild wood I did lie,
A child—with a most knowing eye. (128)

Interestingly, he does not pronounce his first word but lisps it, in a way that recalls the lisping voice of William Wilson's double.[12] Because of the valences of interpretation attached to "lie," the word "eye" also resounds with meaning, and can operate as a *jeu de mot* that reflects all three of the overtones of "lie"—sex, voice, and death. The sexual self ("eye") appears in phallic metonymy (and is, hence, "knowing" in the sexual sense); the self of the voice constitutes the eye ("I") as speaking voice; the self that is aware of his existence recognizes in the "knowing" eye the "I" that will die.

That lying forms an accomplished discourse for Poe becomes most evident, perhaps, in "For Annie." The speaker tells us many times that he is lying. For instance, Poe equates lying with the capacity of fancy, and lying occurs as the speaker drowns in a bath of Annie's hair. More significantly, though, Poe extends the pun in the second stanza, in which the speaker informs us that he can "lie at full length." Given the ambiguity of the first stanza, in which someone (it could be Annie or the narrator) has just passed some ontological boundary (it could be life or death), the "lie" in the second stanza presents particular cognitive exacerbations. Similarly, in describing sleep, the speaker could be engaging in the literal act of reclining, or in the sexual act of "dying." Here Poe describes the deep sleep in the poem:

She tenderly kissed me,
    She fondly caressed,
And then I fell gently
    To sleep on her breast—
Deeply to sleep
    From the heaven of her breast. (458)

Lying as a strategy encodes the meaning for sleep here. Lest Poe's joke that he can tell a deconstructive whopper of a lie be missed, he pushes the pun further:

> . . . I lie at full length—
> But no matter!—I feel
>   I am better at length. (456)

He is better "at length" sexually, ontologically (better because dead and without grief), and strategically, in his use of language, because he can execute from that position his program for rubbing out language—that is, decomposing. To lie at full length for Poe becomes tantamount to finding, in any given poem he constructs, that shifting signifier in his ongoing breviary of contiguous names, and to say it until the poem finally seizes up. It is a kind of one-upmanship, to snuff out one's own poem before someone else can, to play dead—or play alive, depending upon which side of the ambiguity one wishes to play—by lying to one's full extent.

    Thus we see how Poe orients himself in relation to the terms of his poem and the terms *in* his poem, for every term becomes suspect because it is pronounced by one who lies. Certainly he accords that disposition of language to his signifiers proper that are the names of women who are both alive and dead, but Poe moreover registers that hesitancy for all his words in that the subject position of his speaker is one of lying. Possibly Poe's technique for undoing language forms a literary defense mechanism, a protective posture he takes against potentially hostile readers or critics. That posture forms as much the matter of "For Annie" as any romance can. He plays ontological hide-and-seek with the reader. He suggests he lies so convincingly,

> That any beholder
>   Might fancy me dead—
> Might start at beholding me,
>   Thinking me dead. (456)

Start and stop, alive and dead: if we as readers engage with the text, it will die on us; if we mourn, it will pop back alive. The best we can do with Poe, and perhaps all we can do, is to pronounce his list of proper signifiers—not to pronounce them dead or alive, but simply to pronounce them as signifiers—and be left with the bare name of the poem at hand—in this case, "Annie."

    The penultimate stanza demonstrates the speaker's shifting speaker orientation, hinting also that lying is a function of composition.

> And I lie so composedly,
>   Now, in my bed,
> (Knowing her love)
>   That you fancy me dead—(459)

The above lines of decomposition show the speaker parrying his illusion of love with the perceived encroachment of the reader. Lying "composedly" means playing possom in the subject position: the speaker orients himself in the position of desiring subject while pretending to death, a state that utterly precludes desire. The strategy of lying leaves readers with a signifier, repeating obsessively "Annabel Lee" or "Annie"; for example, the final five lines of the poem bear the name "Annie" no less than three times, and the very last word announces the signifier in a way that emphasizes it as the only clutch in an amazingly passive poem, spoken, as it were, from the sofa or bier:

> For it [my heart] sparkles with Annie—
> It glows with the light
> Of the love of my Annie—
> With the thought of the light
> Of the eyes of my Annie. (459)

"Annie" remains the only reason for the poem—and not Annie the person, but "Annie" the intensive and legended signifier, the "Annie" possessed by the narrator.

One final poem, "A Valentine," instances Poe's program of lying in that the poet buries the legended or en-graved signifier in such a fragmented way that we can barely perceive it. The dedication in some versions provides no help, introducing only a blank, "To ———." However, biographical information supplies the observation that Poe sent the Valentine poem to his friend and possible paramour, Frances Sargent Locke Osgood, and with such information, the search for the signifier quickens. Poe tantalizes us, his audience, as he does in "For Annie," in which he keeps the reader guessing whether he exists as alive or dead, and whether Annie herself is alive or dead. Similarly, the signifier in "A Valentine" again offers a woman's name, and like many of his beloveds she demonstrates a gruesome vitality in her "luminous eyes." For her he writes, or rather for her signifier, making clear to her that she

Shall find her own sweet name that, nestling, lies
Upon this page, enwrapped from every reader . . . (389; version G)

He so thoroughly en-graves the name within the poem as to render it almost beyond resuscitation, and at the same time he emphasizes that the signifier is deception: her "sweet name that, nestling, lies." Poe continues to taunt us by asserting that there exists a "treasure" for which we must "search well"; he teases us when he goes so far, at one point, as to tell us to "Cease trying!," concluding with the provocative line: "You will not read the riddle, though you do the best you *can* do" (390). He so defends himself against the reader that we nearly miss the one thing he knows how to say, the signifier for the female name. He spares no pains to accentuate absence:

> And yet there is in this no Gordian knot
> Which one might not undo without a sabre . . . (390)

The "knot" operates as both the confluence of meaning and the absence of meaning ("not") imbedded in the word and surrounding it in asseverations of negation. Notice the superabundance of terms of lack in these two lines: *no, k(not), not, undo, without.*

Poe, unabashed in admitting his strategy of lying, toys with us, preying upon our preconceptions of language as composition, not unlike the manner in which Montresor stalks Fortunato in "The Cask of Amontillado." Though we may start reading Poe's poetry with a preconception of language as composition, we must end with a perception of an itinerary of signifier that instead signals loss. Not above purposely sidetracking us in our search for signifier, he delights in claiming the lie:

> Eyes scintillating soul, there lie *perdus*
> Three eloquent words oft uttered in the hearing
> Of poets, by poets—as the name is a poet's, too. (390)

Of course the poet's name is Osgood's, but at first glance the "three eloquent words" seem to be the ones "oft uttered" lying "*perdus*" right here—that is, the three iterations of "Poe" secreted in the thrice repeated "poets" of the line above: "Of poets, by poets—as the name is a poet's, too."[13] For a moment it seems the poet can only, in the most tautological and solipsistic way, name himself.

He has another name to say, however, as we know by now, the name of the legended beloved, the Annie or Annabel Lee or Helen that displaces one with the other from poem to poem in contiguous obsession, the name that orients the speaker toward his desire for a language always becoming undone. Unlike others of his "love" poems, in which he repeats the signifier for effect, in "A Valentine" he vivisects the signifier, burying it to revive it as we comprehend the acrostic. The acrostic, unconventional and ingenious, uses the first letter of the first line, the second letter of the second line, and so on, to spell out "Frances Sargent Osgood" (Mabbott 390). Similarly, the poem "An Enigma" contains a buried acrostic of the name "Sarah Anna Lewis." In a way reminiscent of alchemists' attraction to secret writing, Poe scatters the signifier in bits among the lines, and locates a desire both playful and ghoulish, thus enacting decomposition and regeneration with a twist.

Poe's agenda privileges the lie—lying down to die, lying in prurient dark bliss next to his chosen signifier, lying at full length to deceive the reader. He lies so he can say the one thing he knows how to say, that death is desire and desire is undoing. In the final quatrain of "A Valentine," Poe describes his engraved signifier:

Its letters, although naturally lying
    Like the knight Pinto—Mendez Ferdinando—
Still form a synonym for Truth.—(390)

As a fascinating aside, the character Mendez Ferdinando found fame for being a liar.[14] The word "form" can suggest a noun as well as a verb, which would render "still form" readable as either "yet compose" or "dead body." In the end, Poe fears most of all that he will find "Still form" to be "a synonym for Truth." In other words, he fears that he will find death to be the only reality, and perhaps concomitantly, silence the only language. Against this, in a seemingly endless concatenation of women's names, he can manage to "lie" in his desires.

CHAPTER 5

Word, Birth, and Whitman's Water Cure

Some of Walt Whitman's most memorable poems utilize the transgression of the maternal embodied in the image of the ocean, and thereby find the "float" of gestative possibility; the speaker of such Whitman poems is possibly never so rapt as when he speaks from a position during which the water of the sea laves his body. In this chapter I examine "Out of the Cradle Endlessly Rocking," "As I Ebb'd with the Ocean of Life," and "Crossing Brooklyn Ferry" as poems celebrating the maternal "float"; first, however, I turn to the conception of the float of parturitive drives and pulsions as it manifests in hydropathy, a movement with widespread adherents in the nineteenth century. Hydropathy, or the water-cure treatment, a pervasive influence in Whitman's America and, particularly, in Whitman's New York, proved, as a therapy dependant on self-reliance, trust in the body, and democratic methods, to possess much to entice the poet.

Whitman's interest in the process of childbirth developed at least in part because of his familiarity with the alternative medical movement of hydropathy. The *Water-Cure Journal* concerned itself as a matter of course with issues of women's health, "consciously citing the cultural connection between 'woman's character and her nurturant roles and responsibilities' " (Cayleff 66). Whitman's awareness of hydropathy was probably spurred by the interest in hydropathy of his publishers, Fowler and Wells. Fowler and Wells distributed the first edition of *Leaves of Grass* in 1855, and published the second edition in 1856; in 1842, states Sherry Ceniza, "Orson S. and Lorenzo N. Fowler took over the editorship of the *American Phrenological Journal* and; in 1848, the *Water-Cure Journal*," and Whitman "read both journals, and both supported woman's rights reform" (47). The *Water-Cure Journal and Herald of Reforms* boasted tens of thousands of subscribers in 1851, throughout the 1850s, and projected 100,000 subscribers by 1860, equaling altogether over one million readers (Cayleff 26). Needless to say, given these figures, hydropathy existed as no mere cult but as an estimable force in medical and cultural movements in antebellum United States.

In addition to reading the *Water-Cure Journal*, Whitman knew several of the most prominent proponents of the water cure, such as Mary Gove Nichols, Russell Trall, Paulina Wright Davis, and Mary Chilton, a water cure physician. Indeed, Whitman's involvement may have proved yet more acute given that water cure treatments were especially popular in New York, Whitman's state of residency. Jane Donegan asserts that "it was in New York that water cure gained its American introduction, produced its major theorists and physicians, gained an enthusiastic following, founded the earliest and some of the largest water-cure establishments, and opened both of its coeducational medical schools" (xiii).

The water cure itself consisted of various applications of pure, as opposed to mineral, usually cold, as opposed to hot (though sometimes tepid or warm) water. The water could be applied in wet sheet packs, or in several manners of soaking, including the sitz bath. Running water also could be used in showers or hosing. Hydropathists urged both external and internal applications: drinking pure water was deemed essential to good health. Understood as a universal cure for all disease and discomfort, water, taken along with a healthy regimen of clean air, simple diet, exercise, and the wearing of loose-fitting clothing, could restore virtually any patient to well-being. In regards to these ministrations, of course, education was indispensible, and the emphasis placed upon self-treatment was paramount. The water cure, thus, appealed to those who preferred to turn not to a medical establishment—at the time highly suspect because of its overwrought usage of measures such as bleeding and lead dosing—but to turn rather to self-sufficiency in treating personal ailment.

Many aspects of the rhetoric of hydropathy would have attracted Whitman; he would have harkened in particular to the insistence upon a patient's autonomy—the stress laid upon teaching that strays from the teacher, to paraphrase the poet. Hydropathy could be practiced at water-cure establishments or at home, so long as the client was willing to educate himself or herself by way of the *Water-Cure Journal* or other water-cure text.[1] A kind of democracy of health care, each human possessing equal rights to the means of his or her way to health regardless of social class, water cure therapy implicitly supported a practice wherein the medicine—water—was available to everyone. The therapy also linked itself with the cause of temperance, a cause Whitman espoused, notably with the publication of his temperance novel, *Franklin Evans*, and the movement elicited "conversion" narratives extolling the wonders of water treatment. In addition to these characteristics of self-reliance, temperance, and ecstatic conversion, hydropathy advocated a belief in the body's basic health and perfectibility, a frank acceptance of sexuality, and an almost spiritual relationship with water as the elixir of life. All of these attributes Whitman embraced; David Reynolds, for example, suggests that Whitman's "exhilarating plunge into the ocean—'Cushion me soft, rock me in billowy drowse,/ Dash me with amorous wet, I can repay you"—is a giddy rendition of water cure therapy, which he had been advising since the *Eagle* days" (332–33).

Whitman would have been drawn, moreover, to one further attribute—hydropathy's attention to women's health, and childbirth in particular. Hydropathy concentrated especially on the concerns of female medicine such as prenatal care, labor, childbirth, and postpartum activity. Women's power over their parturition allowed them to bypass the sometimes heavyhanded ministrations of allopathic physicians, and the sometimes amateurish attentions of the new male midwives, whose services had begun in the middle of the nineteenth century to dominate the field.

The *Water-Cure Journal* is replete with accounts of satisfactory and even glowing parturitive experiences as a result of water treatments, the most common being the tepid sitz bath, used for relaxation, dilation, alleviation of contractions, and other desirable responses. The journal was often explicit about details of parturition, from which the poet might have gleaned information. For instance, in a June 29, 1847, piece, "A Case of Childbirth, and Management of the New-Born Child," details of delivery are clear: "Labor came unexpectedly upon her," the report states, "she supposing herself to be at the end of the eighth month. The labor was rather tedious . . ." (179). The report proceeds to state that the woman drank water (cold) "abundantly," bathed, and "wore a wet girdle during the night" (179) for several nights, and underwent more baths, and that full strength returned in three or four days.

Hydropathy proponents such as Mary Gove Nichols argued against the mainstream allopathic procedures whereby pregnancy was treated as a disease, urging control of women's bodies by women themselves. To water cure advocates, "with their abiding faith in the ability of the individual to control her own destiny," states Donegan, "the increasing professionalization of childbirth and the patient's concomitant abrogation of responsibility were anathema" (85). While both men and women in great numbers used water cures, it may well be that the movement affected women more profoundly because it redefined their position culturally and individually—and beyond issues only of physical health. Cayleff states the matter as follows:

Because of the way hydropaths viewed disease (as a systemic disorder in which nature and external life conditions had gone awry), they did not counterattack by assigning the patient a passive role; instead, they chose to modify the life conditions of the ill person. This outlook served to expand women's control over their lives. . . . For women, then, the tenets of hydropathy offered the opportunity to redefine their physiological processes, control their medical care and, ultimately, expand their social roles and opportunities. No other nineteenth-century sect offered such an all-encompassing, accessible, and empowering medical and social ideology. (16)

Thus women's understanding of their own bodies underwent an exhilarating and powerful change, and their attitude toward childbearing became more active and centered in the experience of the self. Danielson, too, attributes the understanding of social conditions as a factor in women's health, asserting that water cure approaches "base prescriptions for health on a belief that social conditions, not physiological characteristics, cause female disabilities, and that a change in those conditions will allow women's natural capacity for nurturance to express itself in the roles of wife and mother, physician and minister" (248).

A pride in women's physiology attended these new attitudes, with lecturers such as Paulina Wright Davis speaking with candor about the female body. Editor William Elder in the *Water-Cure Journal* recommended Davis as a fine scientist: "'Provided with the best substitutes for actual dissection which art has been able to supply . . . [and] with the aid of that wonderful machine, the *modelle du femme*, capital life-sized plates, and such dry preparations as our anatomical museums afford, I regard her, for all purposes except practical surgery, as a complete anatomist'" (cited in Ceniza 100). Whitman attended lectures such as those given by Paulina Wright Davis, read her works, met with her at the home of Abby Hills Price, and had an opportunity to visit her in 1868 at her home in Providence (Ceniza 99; 136).

Whitman knew, read, and attended to the works not only of Paulina Wright Davis, but also of Mary Gove Nichols and Russell Trall, all active in the hydropathy movement. Almost certainly, Whitman also knew of Mary Gove Nichols from the *Water-Cure Journal*. Paulina Wright Davis mailed a copy of *Leaves of Grass* to Mary Gove Nichols in June 1875; both of these reforming women probably saw Whitman's poetry as "a text supporting their own texts" (Ceniza 102); all three were active in redefining female options in the nineteenth century. Too, Whitman almost certainly knew of Russell Trall who, like the poet, published with Fowler and Wells.

Russell Trall must have captivated Whitman with his straightforward discussions of passion, sexuality, and athleticism. Reynolds draws parallels between Trall and Whitman because Trall "treated sex frankly and yet firmly denounced both pornography and bad language"; similarly, Whitman, in *Leaves of Grass*, presented himself "as one familiar with slang but avoiding obscenity, comfortable with sex but skirting pornography" (208–9). Both could be explicit and still cleanly in their representations of physiology. Russell Trall disbelieved in women's "'passionlessness,'" claiming equal pleasure in sex for both men and women: "'It is true that the sexual orgasm on the part of the female is just as normal as on the part of the male'" (cited in Cayleff 57); women's erotic desires were just as admissable as men's and, according to Trall, the sex act performed at all deserved to be performed well.

In his 1857 *The Illustrated Family Gymnasium*, published by Fowler and Wells, Trall advocated exercise for nineteenth-century women he perceived as enervated because of Victorian standards of decorum, and offered illustrations of women lifting barbells (Reynolds 217). Whitman's Amazonian women in "Children of Adam" seem not unlike these strong women, portrayed as maternal strongholds and effective childbearers, as antidote to the contemporaneous fear that powerful mothers had become compromised by enervated health. Russell Trall was adamant that noninterventionist health care provided the cure for disease and distress, and specified the inclusion of childbirth as a state of health; for Trall, a woman who suffered agonies during childbirth was a woman who had defied the laws of natural care of the body. He believed that an expectant mother who followed the tenets of hydropathy had no need to fear pain—an inducement, perhaps, for the poet, who took on the female role of giving birth.

Enjoying the boast of perfect health, Whitman may have imagined his speaker, laved in water, birthed by the sea-mother of erotic birth contractions and ecstatic delivery. Utilizing information about water cure methods, with which his nineteenth-century readers would have been familiar, Whitman played on readers' expectations of health by portraying labor and delivery in the most dramatic hydropathic environment of all—the sea. Taking on his role as mother man, Whitman surrounded himself with water and transgressed the maternal to deliver an impassioned word out of the sea. The water cure backgrounding for the poems discussed below remains essential to their success, the natal imperative for Whitman undeniable, the position of water nearly omnipresent.

On Christmas Eve 1859, the New York *Saturday Press* published a Whitman poem titled "A Child's Reminiscence." While the date of December 24 may be a coincidence, it may be that the editor, Henry Clapp, judged the subject in the poem to be apropos to the occasion of Christmas Eve. It may also be that Whitman, far from diffident about promoting his own work, urged his friend, Clapp, to print "A Child's Reminiscence" because Whitman thought the poem's themes would be shown to best effect by a Christmas debut. Whereas the date of Christmas Day would have prompted a recollection of the baby Jesus, that of Christmas Eve prompted a focus on the activities of the mother, so that the holiday may highlight the mother Mary and the poem's maternal bias.[2] The date, the evening before Mary gives birth to baby Jesus, offers a fitting backdrop for a poem that depends not only upon the child but expressly upon the maternal.[3]

Whitman revised "A Child's Reminiscence" in 1860 and retitled it "A Word out of the Sea," a useful title, as the saying of the one word, given by the maternal sea, provides the ultimate gift of the poem. The poem depicts a gift, given by a mother character, the sea—borne by her, actually—in the form of a word. The introduction to the 1859 poem in the *Saturday Press* may well have been written by Whitman: "Our readers may, if they choose, consider as our Christmas or New Year's present to them, the curious warble, by Walt Whitman, of 'A Child's Reminiscence' on our First Page" (Whitman, *Collected Writings* 246) .[4] Whitman gives to the reader the gift of a word from the ultimate mother on the most maternal evening in our culture: Merry Christmas out of the semiotic realm.[5]

The poem was further revised by Whitman in 1871 and given the title with which we are more familiar, "Out of the Cradle Endlessly Rocking," a title more perspicacious yet, as it too pinpoints the maternal by association with "cradle," and further suggests womblike pulsions in the word "rocking." Almost at random we find lines that portray the *choric* repetitions in the poem, as it rocks us back to the maternal mode. From many possible examples, the repetitions of the word "carols" serve here:

Shake out carols!
Solitary here, the night's carols!
Carols of lonesome love! death's carols!
Carols under that lagging, yellow, waning moon!
O under that moon where she droops almost down into the sea!
O reckless despairing carols. (246)

In this one example, chosen nearly randomly from manifold possibilities of womb pulsions and cradle-rocking rhythms, the mesmeric repetition educes the maternal realm.

Whitman utilizes other feminine poetic traits in the poem, too. The preposition "out," which initiates the title, alludes, tantalizingly, to something that the poem will deliver, but doesn't specify (as the 1860 title blatantly does—namely, "a word"). The first three lines show a correspondence between mother and music: "Out of the cradle endlessly rocking,/ Out of the mocking-bird's throat, the musical shuttle,/ Out of the Ninth-month midnight" (246). The parataxis in the repetition of "out" sets up the congruence of birth and maternally induced song. That this is a mother's poem proves undeniable. Most strikingly, the 1860 version announces its topic with the unequivocal first line, "Out of the mother's womb, and from the nipples of her breast."

The paired poems "Out of the Cradle" and "As I Ebbed with the Ocean of Life" will provide the encapsulating poems for this chapter on Whitman's naming and the water cure. The poems provide quintessential examples of *chora* in Whitman's ultimate canon of *chora*; accordingly, I use them to explore Whitman's poems of maternal poetics and naming. This chapter also focuses specifically on the image of the "float," as evoked in those poems and "Crossing Brooklyn Ferry." Whitman's usage of the float, generally speaking, can be traced in part an interest in hydropathy, which contextualizes the association of sea poems with birthing poems.

So prevalent are the maternal cues in "Out of the Cradle" that latter twentieth- and early twenty-first-century readers might be tempted to call the poem an experience of "re-birthing." From the earliest parts of the poem Whitman cues us: "Ninth-month," the half-moon "swollen," eggs in the birds' nest, and "the mystic play of shadows twining and twisting as if they were alive." The mystic shadow image recalls the crucial line in "Song of Myself," discussed earlier, which also depends upon shadows as intimations of the embryonic: "Putting myself here and now to the ambushed womb of the shadows!" (Cowley 72). As we have seen, that line tips the import of Whitman's "Song of Myself," announcing his primary poetic concern with ambushing the womb and thereby transgressing the maternal and developing a poetics of the feminine.

The first dramatic movement in "Out of the Cradle" occurs when the female bird disappears, and the mother-principle seems to be lost to the poem: "One forenoon the she-bird crouch'd not on the nest."[6] No reason is given for her disappearance, but it becomes manifest that "Out of the Cradle" cannot exist without the mother, for as soon as we know the she-bird never "appear'd again," the mother principle immediately intimates itself, in the next line, " . . . thenceforward all summer in the sound of the sea" (248). Though the reader does not know yet that the ocean will establish itself as the maternal force that builds to a parturitive climax, still the reader can sense it early on in this line. The ocean's song promptly becomes a force and thereafter gathers power. It takes some time for the ocean as mother actually to become a character but her incarnation has been made apparent; a kind of transubstantiation, almost, begins to take place, from bird-mother to sea-mother, and from this point following, the sound of the ocean begins to amplify. Sonically, the volume of ocean noise—the waves and drives of the maternal—rises in the mix of the poem, to crescendo in the final parts.

The loss of the mother bird occasions the song of the male bird, whose voice will dominate the middle sections of the poem before the mother voice resumes. I will return to that resuming crescendo but wish to consider for a moment a comparison of Whitman's and Poe's scenes of the birth of language, because of the light they might shed ultimately on Whitman's feminine poetics. If we think of Poe's "The Raven" as forerunner to "Out of the Cradle," some elements begin to sound acutely familiar.[7] For instance, the Poe-esque overtones of melancholy, stillness, and compulsion dominate the following:

For somewhere I believe I heard my mate responding to me,
So faint, I must be still, be still to listen,
But not altogether still, for then she might not come immediately to me. (108–10)

Equally important, "Out of the Cradle" parallels "The Raven" in the way the authors configure the characters: in both poems the lost mother appears in the guise of another character (Lenore as mother in Poe's poem, she-bird as sea-mother in Whitman's). In both poems the bird occupies a familial relationship with the narrator; the bird functions as a father figure in Poe's poem, and a "brother" in Whitman's. In both a bird with parrot-like qualities attempts to teach the main character the signifier; Poe chooses the raven for these qualities, and Whitman the mockingbird.

It is impossible not to notice, furthermore, that Whitman's bird is precisely a *mocking*bird, and as such, a curious choice as the teacher of the signifier. Both poems need the bird in order to prompt the narrator's entry into signification. The implication for both poets remains that the bird actually may be repeating rather than initiating the signifier, an apt circumstance, given that entry into the realm of signification can never be an original experience; language has always already existed, and it is the case that the signifier constitutes the speaker, rather than that the speaker discovers signification. In other words, language speaks the subject and not the other way around.

Mark Bauerlein suggests that the narrator doesn't join in the song but instead painstakingly records it; he "translates" it (143), a somewhat reluctant activity that recalls that of the student in "The Raven," also reticent to enter the symbolic mode. Poe's narrator—falling short of the example of the raven who could "quoth" the signifier—never quite says the signifier himself. The boy in "Out of the Cradle," too, only translates but doesn't himself sing. Occasionally, this translating of the mockingbird finds the poem in trouble, especially where

Whitman seems to stage a recording of a recording—truly a mocking. Such a predicament can reverberate in nearly endless echoes, as in the following:

Do not be decoy'd elsewhere,
That is the whistle of the wind, it is not my voice,
That is the fluttering of the spray,
Those are the shadows of leaves. (250–51)

Decoying, whistling, fluttering, shadows: this recording is additionally complicated by the competing sounds of the wind and the sea. The one who sings here is the bird, the teacher of the signifier, but even his voice can be confused by the young boy. The mocking can be mistaken for a decoy, which might be the wind's whistle or the sea spray's flutter, for the bird needs to clarify: "*it is not my voice.*" Making sure that the bird's voice is heard for itself, even though it is a mocking voice, is essential, the bird says, but given all the multilayered sounds, discernment of the bird's voice could be a tough assignment. Too, the bird warns against what might become Whitman's own voice: not the leaves but the shadows of leaves, not the writing but the decoy of the writing. The bird warns the boy to retain the basic natural rhythms and not to be fooled by imitations of rhythms.

As in "The Raven," the oedipal triad is important. Poe presents the bird, the speaker, and the mother (Pallas); Whitman presents the bird, the speaker, and the mother (sea). Bauerlein points out that song in Whitman's poem proves unsuccessful because it doesn't resuscitate the dead female bird; the song "fails to achieve its specific purpose—to return the 'she-bird to her lover' " (147–48). I would point out similarly that in Poe's poem, the raven's word, "Nevermore," cannot bring Lenore back to life. Though both birds may prove ineffectual at raising the dead through stating the signifier, it is not for lack of trying, repeatedly.

The birds prove masters of repetition, and in the case of Whitman's mockingbird the usages of repetition become almost myriad. In Whitman's lines we hear a clear allusion to Poe's repetition of "Nevermore," the "never more" anticipated in "no more," earlier on in the poem: "*We two together no more*" (251), but fully realized a little further on, with repetitions of "never more":

O you singer solitary, singing by yourself, projecting me,
O solitary me listening, never more shall I cease perpetuating you,
Never more shall I escape, never more the reverberations,
Never more the cries of unsatisfied love be absent from me,
Never again leave me to be the peaceful child I was before what there in the night,
By the sea under the yellow and sagging moon,
The messenger there arous'd, the fire, the sweet hell within,
The unknown want, the destiny of me. (252)

"Never more" intones with Whitmanian rhythm the Poe signifier; "Never more the reverberations" shall be absent from the speaker once he becomes born into the symbolic realm. Whitman's "never more" can be disturbing, as in "the cries of unsatisfied love" that the intonation of "never more" cannot assuage, but unlike Poe he embraces the loss. For both poets the loss occasions the discovery of song, the *différence* where language might start.

Something more complex, however, than simply Poe's "nevermore" occurs here. The "no more" of the earlier line may herald the mother's emergence four lines later as a full presence in the poem, preempting the bird, for as the "aria [of the bird is] sinking," the sea-mother's song starts to rise: "With angry moans the fierce old mother incessantly moaning" (251). Betsy Erkkila points out that the sea becomes a major character in the above line, contending that, "here for the first time the 'fierce old mother' the sea, whose 'angry moans' have surged as a hoarse undercurrent through the poem, joins the boy and the bird to become a major character in the drama; it is she who bears the 'drowned secret' suspected by the bird, sought by the boy, and translated by the poet" (172). The fierce mother—a slap in the face of the nineteenth-century "cult of the mother" as the serene angel of the house—moans, a word possibly connoting sexuality but in this case also the sounds of birthing. A form of the word "moan" occurs twice in the line above, forcing attention upon the sound, and the word "incessantly," used to describe the mother's moaning, catches up the connotations of "endlessly" in the title.

With her moans of labor pain, the sea singing, and the yellow half-moon sagging and drooping so as almost to touch the sea with her full belly, Whitman gives us a landscape of the maternal. He further enhances the scene of birthing with the graphic depiction of the mother's body, her "liquid rims and wet sands." From the mother's body the word issues, and also from it the boy issues; it is not the mother's mouth, but the mother's body that whispers. As pertains to Lacanian theory, the boy may be misguided, for he seeks the word from the mother rather than seeking the name from the father when he asks,

A word then, (for I will conquer it,)
The word final, superior to all,
Subtle, sent up—what is it?—I listen;
Are you whispering it, and have been all the time, you sea-waves?
Is that it from your liquid rims and wet sands? (252)

The sea mother has been whispering it all along throughout the course of the poem, and it is only one word—actually, more rhythm than word, from her liquid rims, from out of her body.

The word "Death" works as a kind of mantra to abate the anxiety of loss, which Whitman designates as the superior word, for it facilitates birth, especially at the poem's conclusion, in which the sea whispers him, and the boy is born into language. In this regard, Larson notes that "Out of the Cradle" attempts to "restage the epiphanic emergence of discourse" (186); Warren goes further, offering the observation that the poem delivers the one word, the meaning of which "is implied by the comforting tone of the stanza, but it remains a translation of an unknown tongue. The central absence of defined meaning is the source of more words, more songs" (166). The signifier "Death" marks both an ending and a beginning, and dramatizes the boy's entry, heralded by loss, into a web of signifiers that will for the man, Whitman, be the source of more songs.

I suggest a slightly different turn to the scenario than that offered by Larson and Warren, and that is this: the boy does wish to enter into the economy of the signifier as shown to him by the bird (father's) song, but he also wishes to reclaim the drives of the mother's body, the rhythms that underlie his verse. Contrapuntal, the poem needs both the desire *à la lettre* and the yearning for maternal pulsions to show the boy as the particular kind of "outsetting bard" who will travel both forward into signification and lean backward into the womb's *choric* rhythms in order for his voice to emerge. Interestingly, he can translate the bird, but he cannot quite translate the sea: "Subtle, sent up—what is it?—I listen" (252). The mother is reticent, as opposed to the bird, whose signifiers dominate the poem—especially the signifier, "Loved! loved! loved! loved! loved!" (251).

Though the mother presumably whispers one word, she concomitantly "whispers" a body. An immaculate birth of *écriture féminine*, what happens on the beach both endorses language with the signifier, and confounds language with the body. That Whitman can move in both directions at once—language and body, signifier and *chora*—in the one whisper from the liquid rims, provides powerful testimony to his belief in the maternal body. The maternal landscape appears again and again in the poem. Whitman evokes the womb-space specifically in the night beach scene:

For more than once dimly down to the beach gliding,
Silent, avoiding the moonbeams, blending myself with the shadows,
Recalling now the obscure shapes, the echoes, the sounds and sights after their sorts
   . . . (249)

The presence of shadows, again, indicates the ambushed womb, Whitman may be trying to understand the fetus as an organism that replicates its parents, reproducing their genes, "after their sorts." What the child does is to listen—he "Listen'd long and long"—and the reason he listens is in order to be able to find the scaffolding of rhythm for his song.

In the 1860 version of the poem, Whitman adds the lines, "Elemental drifts!/ O I wish I could impress others as you and the waves have just been impressing me" (Whitman, *Collected Writings* 318). The pun contained in the word "im-press" serves to dignify and privilege the role of bodily *choric* pulsions in developing utterance. Ultimately, Whitman wants the Whitmanian song to unfold from the mother's folds of pressings and pulsings at the same time that it designates itself by the Name-of-the-Father signifier. The birthing mother in her "whispers" imports the narrator into life: she brings the narrator into being as she brings the poet into being. The mother ocean, the most generative character in the poem, effects undulations that offer restorative properties, so that each "*wave soothes the wave behind,*" "*embracing and lapping*" (249).

Offering her bounty of "some drown'd secret hissing" (251), she drives and pulses him. Indeed, the entire dynamic of the poem indicates a parturient experience, from the point of view of the boy. That is, the baby almost seems to describe its own birth. An astonishing aspect of "Out of the Cradle" remains the fact that the poem not only has a feminine landscape of womb-space, it very often *is* that space. If it is too much to say that at its most powerful and encrypted points the poem unfolds from the point of view of the fetus, nevertheless it may at the very least be said that the poem accrues to itself the ambience of maternal drives and repetitions in order to enact the particular milieu of parturition. Whitman draws from the maternal, his writing powerful because of its feminine poetics.

As with the speaking position of a newly arriving infant, the boy hasn't yet entered the symbolic mode and still hasn't completely exited the semiotic. Much has been made of Whitman's attention to the realistic and naturalistic attributes of the song of the bird, but I would like to point out, in addition, how well Whitman attends to the song of the body of the mother.[8] The line "Creeping thence steadily up to my ears and laving me softly all over" (253) approximates the amniotic ambience of the *in utero* state, the speaker turning in the womb, before delivery at the end of the next and final stanza, in which the sea whispers him. The sea in "Out of the Cradle" personifies a mother who delivers the boy in the final line: "The sea whisper'd me" (253). In some ways the entire poem forms a portrayal of parturition, with the objective being the delivery of the boy, with the climax in the ultimate line.

As the sea begins to whisper the boy into life, she also lisps "the low and delicious word death" (252). She lisps it to the boy and it is her only word, distinguished not so much in the meaning or the saying of it, but in its sound. Interestingly, there are no quotation marks around the word to emphasize its status as signifier, and no italics, as in the case of all the bird's signifiers. Rather, the word's import derives from its repetition. Death is the answer the sea gives to the question about the "word final," that the sea whispers from her liquid rims and wet sands, the word existing as much as pulsions and rhythms as it does word. The mother answers by whispering the boy into being and at the same time lisping death:

And again death, death, death, death,
Hissing melodious, neither like the bird nor like my arous'd child's heart,
But edging near as privately for me rustling at my feet,
Creeping thence steadily up to my ears and laving me softly all over,
Death, death, death, death, death. (252–53)

The melodious hissing remains the most memorable sound in these lines, the pulsing of the sea's answer the most perspicacious factor. The nature of her utterance distinguishes itself from the nature of the bird's song, the mother's utterance remaining private and bodily, bold and rhythmic, laving the boy's body. The word of the sea-mother exists as touch, the texture of water, a motion.

In fact, the speaker needs both the utterance of the bird and the sea to make his own songs, both the rhythms of the *chora* and the naming of the signifier, semiotic and symbolic together. He makes clear that he must fuse the lisp of the sea and the song of the demon or bird. He claims the hissing of the sea,

Which I do not forget,
But fuse the song of my dusky demon and brother,
That he sang to me in the moonlight on Paumanok's gray beach,
With the thousand responsive songs at random,
My own songs awaked from that hour . . . (253)

He needs the song of the bird—the male voice—but he also needs the hissing of the sea—the maternal rhythms—in order to be able to find himself as a poet potent with both paternal voice and female pulsion. The signifier is mighty but in Whitman even more mighty is the ability to yearn and harken to the maternal from which rhythm arises.

The extent to which the mother figure holds a place of importance in Whitman's poetry has been largely underrated, for a major force in Whitman's poetics proves not only the masculine phallic thrust but the feminine laboring push. Whitman's writing of the mother's body at times sounds much like the *écriture féminine* elucidated more than a century later—a type of writing that depends upon the white ink of milk and the *jouissance* of gestation. He rewards readings of his feminine poetics the more we document and expand upon them, rhythmic intensity underlying his most successful language experiments—an intensity that remains expressly female.

Vivian Pollak and others have observed that feminist readings of Whitman remain far from numerous and are greatly needed in offering a full range of Whitman scholarship. Pollak, notably, has contributed fine observations about Whitman's women as mothers and examines "both Whitman's feminism and his antifeminism, his resistance to linguistically totalizing norms, and his reaffirmation of the mid-nineteenth-century American cult of the mother, which celebrated maternity as any woman's supreme destiny" ("Visionary" 92). Her book, *The Erotic Whitman*, and Ceniza's *Walt Whitman and 19th-Century Women Reformers*, have launched the investigation of the influence of women and the feminine on Whitman's poetry and, despite their fine studies, much more work remains to be done.

The extent to which Whitman draws on the feminine ranges throughout his *oeuvre*: "Out of the Cradle" is far from the only maternal poem of Whitman's. I mention briefly here several poems that likewise draw on the maternal before I continue the foregoing discussion by addressing "As I Ebb'd," the companion poem to "Out of the Cradle." Notably, "The Sleepers" resolves in the plenary images of the speaker being yielded forth, or born, from the mother:

I will duly pass the day O my mother and duly return to you
Not you will yield forth the dawn again more surely than you will yield forth me
   again,
Not the womb yields the babe in its time more surely than I shall be yielded from
   you in my time. (Cowley 115)

The repetition of the word "yield" and its forms proves notable. The poem ends with the limber syntax that gives Whitman a womb, or rather, *makes* Whitman a womb, for syntactically they are equated; emphatically, this poem, like "Out of the Cradle," limns the process of one experiencing birth. Whitman chose, interestingly, to suppress the 1855 version of "The Sleepers" in the final *Leaves of Grass*, by omitting the last two of the three lines above. Perhaps he worried that he had crossed gender lines too shockingly for his readers, and decided to temper the tone of his maternal urgings.

Whitman fulfills the epithet of mother man that his friend Burroughs designated, and not surprisingly Burroughs wasn't the only friend who saw Whitman so. Edward Carpenter, for example, saw him as "humorous, shrewd, motherly" (6). Whitman displays these characteristics in his farewell song "So Long!," where he celebrates the mother function as his own, listing it as one of his most important accomplishments: "I have sung the body and the soul, war and peace have I sung, and the songs of life and death,/ And the songs of birth and shown that there are many births" (503).

A poet of many births, he focuses in the remarkable short poem "Unseen Buds," on the unborn, the foetus still in gestation. Here follows the poem in full:

Unseen buds, infinite, hidden well,
Under the snow and ice, under the darkness, in every square or cubic inch,
Germinal, exquisite, in delicate lace, microscopic, unborn,
Like babes in wombs, latent, folded, compact, sleeping;
Billions of billions, and trillions of trillions of them waiting,
(On earth and in the sea—the universe—the stars there in the heavens,)
Urging slowly, surely forward, forming endless,
And waiting ever more, forever more behind. (557)

The unborn are everywhere, in countless numbers, trillions of trillions of babes in wombs. Even though they remain hidden, they prove perceptible to the poet; Whitman imposed upon himself as a poet the job of pointing out the unborn babies, the "latent, folded" ones still gestating, and recording their urgings. An unusual, even astonishing, job for a male poet, it stands as one of his major projects, and one of the most distinguishing features of his work.

The maternal urgings in "As I Ebb'd with the Ocean of Life" prove more yearning and nostalgic than those we've discussed so far, though they still augment an understanding of the poet's language experiment. As I turn now to the second poem of the pair that organizes this chapter, I note that "As I Ebb'd" has been seen as one of Whitman's bleakest poems. Full of "melancholy and doubt" (Hutchinson 103), a poem that claims hopeless things in a "bitter deflation" (Nathanson 446), "As I Ebb'd" marks a despondent and self-chastising (Edwin Miller 46–47) stage of Whitman's work; David Cavitch proposes that "As I Ebb'd" stands as the first poem in Whitman's *oeuvre* in which he doesn't transform his shame into something else (21). While this companion poem to "Out of the Cradle" explores despondency, however, it broaches a particular kind of devastation, a kind perhaps necessary for the signifying poet. "As I Ebb'd" tells the story of the onset of the symbolic as experienced by the speaking subject, concomitant with the subject's pain at having had to relinquish the preverbal.[9]

In "Out of the Cradle," the boy most often inhabits the prenaming, semiotic phase, while in "As I Ebb'd" the boy, having attained the signifier, will exist finally in the symbolic, but yearn for the *chora*. Michael Moon discusses the poet's conflict in "As I Ebb'd" as being "in close congruence of both conflict and resolution with Lacan's account of the oedipal crisis from the point of view of the male subject" (144–45), in which he renounces the " 'fluid' identity he has shared with the figure of the mother and, in 'the Name of the Father,' renounces his 'fluid' identity and accepts an oedipalized male one . . . and takes his place in the oedipally ordered fields of language and culture" (145). While I don't see Whitman's renunciation and transformation as quite so complete as Moon does, I view "As I Ebb'd" as offering a paradigm of one who takes his place in the ordered fields of language and culture. The poem, however, is also fraught with the recurrence that seeps through repression, so that *both* verbal and preverbal powers are at work.

Reminiscent of the *choric* waves in "Out of the Cradle," the later poem continues the maternal rhythms in its opening:

As I walk'd where the ripples continually wash you Paumanok,
Where they rustle up hoarse and sibilant,
Where the fierce old mother endlessly cries for her castaways . . . (253)

The hoarseness and sibilance recall the lisp and hiss and husky voice of the sea in "Out of the Cradle," Whitman conflating the two poems with the sound of the ocean-mother's voice. Whereas the ocean laves and covers the boy in amniotic fluid and whispers him into being in the first poem, here she cries for her castaways, one of which is certainly the speaker. He is an outcast from the pulsions of the mother, born and subsequently caught irretrievably in the web of signification, and "Held by this electric self out of the pride of which I utter poems" (253). Even though he is held by the self that utters, because caught in signification's web, he still can be "seiz'd by the spirit that trails in the lines underfoot" (253), the spirit of the maternal patternings of rhythm. The self that utters becomes apprehended from time to time by his memory of rhythmic urgings, for the lines underfoot imply the unconscious or repressed memory of the mother's body. Just as an ocean wave can seize a foot, the feral death-mother of "Out of the Cradle" can seize a speaker (whose voice speaks in poetic feet) existing in the symbolic; she seizes him with the intimations, the memories of her ineluctable pulsions.

The poem induces *choric* lulling by recalling the anaphoric first three lines of "Cradle," each of which begins with the preposition "out"; in "As I Ebb'd" the first three lines also begin anaphorically, with the repetition of "as." The word "out" cues the reader for the movement of delivery, while "as" denotes a stasis or waiting. The hypnotic pulsing sways the reader of "As I Ebb'd" to recall with the speaker the mother's amniotic lullings (and the word "endlessly" in the fifth line also recalls the timeless state of gestation in the earlier poem). The companion poem proves replete with ripples, wash, rustle, sibilance, and also a kind of maternal rocking, but harsher in sound, perhaps more ruptured.

What has happened between "Out of the Cradle" and "As I Ebb'd" is, quite simply, language. The latter poem results from the entry of the speaking subject into the symbolic mode and the presumed career of the speaking subject subsequent to that entry. One of the clues to this change inheres in the fact that the rim now is no longer the ultra feminine "liquid rim" of "Out of the Cradle" but instead that which "stands for" something else—"all the water and all the land of the globe." From his positioning in the symbolic the speaker finds himself yearning to remember the mostly repressed semiotic, to which his eyes are "reverting" (254). They lower their gaze to a visual representation of the aural reality that was the *chora*: he sees windrows, the lines left by the rhythm of the sea. Detritus and chaff and weeds and scum compose the lines, and bring "the old thought of likenesses" (254), which causes the speaker to seek "types" of the basic rhythm. He no longer has direct access to the semiotic but retains recourse to the types of the semiotic in the visual lines of the windrows. Larson observes, to this effect, that the speaker's activity of wandering along the shore actually entails that of looking for a poem: "the speaker continues to patrol the beach, 'miles walking,' in search of the poem whose 'drift' he aims to 'gather'" (198). The speaker tries to find a poem that will conform to his recurrent intuitive or sensate memory, partial though that may be, of basic rhythms of the maternal body. This recurrence sparks his motivation.

This speaker, as in the finale of "Out of the Cradle," exhibits an awareness of self as dependent upon the sea, only here the buoyancy is gone:

I too but signify at the utmost a little wash'd-up drift,
A few sands and dead leaves to gather . . . (254)

The manner in which Whitman employs the verb "signify" can reveal the speaker as either passive or active, as either the thing that means or the one who confers meaning by speaking, even if all he states is drift and sands and dead leaves.[10] The speaker and the speaker's project of signifying has become grounded, disgraced by debris; his project forms a system of "blabs" that the speaker's "real" self mocks with laughter, scorning all he's written:

Aware now that amid all that blab whose echoes recoil upon me I have not once
    had the least idea who or what I am,
But that before all my arrogant poems the real Me stands yet untouch'd, untold, al-
    together unreach'd,
Withdrawn far, mocking me with mock-congratulatory signs and bows,
With peals of distant ironical laughter at every word I have written,
Pointing in silence to these songs, and then to the sand beneath. (254)

If the "real Me" who stands untouched and untold comprises the self before language—that is, the self we saw in "Out of the Cradle"—it would make sense that that real Me mocks the speaking Me by "Pointing in silence to these songs, and then to the sand beneath," because silence remains the only *modus operandum* for the self before language. Moreover, the real Me mocks the speaker by recourse to the memory of the *chora*—"in sight of the sea" where nature comes to "dart upon me and sting me," because he has "dared to open my mouth to sing at all" (254). What stings most, however, is that the real Me can never be regained.

Usually understood as depicting personal despair, these stanzas, I propose, do not register the sting in so personal and idiosyncratic a way, but serve instead to describe the experience of the artist who by needs has become trapped within signification. Many artists must come to terms at some point with the sense of loss prompted by the realization that representation can never substitute for the real, for language has boundaries, after all; the name is not the thing. The poet can be "baffled, balk'd, bent to the very earth" (25) by such a realization—bent as if oppressed, but more poignantly, bent in recognition of his limitations as he examines the wet sand where the windrows represent the non-verbal pulsions of the real. Knowing, as a writer, that one can never return to the real of the semiotic must constitute a chastening experience, but not necessarily a flattening one. The "real Me" laughs at his "every word" because the word appears necessarily in the symbolic and can never be the real, which is something like the "silence," to which the "real Me" points. His preoccupation with representation carries into the next section, in which he realizes that the "little shreds indeed standing for you and me and all" seem but fragments of that for which they stand. The real includes the ocean and the self and the all of the globe, whereas representation can only offer little shreds.

The speaker enters into extremely dangerous territory here, positioning himself between his parents, wanting, as Edwin Haviland Miller points out, his "island-father" to hug him and his "sea-mother" to hold him to her (47). He tries to return to the spot where he first entered the world after the issuance from the semiotic mother and before entry into the symbolic Name-of-the-Father, desiring existence, simultaneously, in both modes. To lie at the point at which the waves wax and ebb would be to lie at the point of sexual contact between sea and earth, between mother and father—the point of conception. Perhaps the desire for this convergence between mother and father is the reason that he may try, in an astonishing gender-blurring, to suckle from the father:

I throw myself upon your breast my father,
I cling to you so that you cannot unloose me,
I hold you firm till you answer me something. (255)

The speaker would wish for the father character to preempt the mother function, in a moment of desperate action, but he cannot bring the moment to its peak. The speaker holds his father firmly and continues to demand particular actions of his father:

Kiss me my father,
Touch me with your lips as I touch those I love,
Breathe to me while I hold you close the secret of the murmuring I envy. (255)

The envied murmuring recalls the inchoate *chora*, even though the person described here is the father and the son wants him to speak an answer, in a moment much more problematic than any in "Song of Myself." In "As I Ebb'd" Whitman attempts to impose the male-mother role in an action by the speaker that is at least desperate and at most almost rapacious.[11]

The 1860 version of "As I Ebb'd" adds an important line: "For I fear I shall become crazed, if I cannot emulate it, and utter myself as well as it" (Bradley Blodgett Golden White 320). The speaker registers desperation in the face of the fact that he now perceives representation as little shreds. Most of all, however, he wishes to merge again with the mother. To alleviate the feared diminishment of the semiotic, he tries to make himself one with the mother as he was in "Out of the Cradle," immersed in the float. In so doing he offers a regression both painful and poignant:

I too have bubbled up, floated the measureless float, and been wash'd on your shores,
I too am but a trail of drift and debris,
I too leave little wrecks upon you, you fish-shaped island. (255)

The speaker has "floated the measureless float," he says, participated in the sensate drives of the mother's body, in an uncalibrated time before language, and this action I take as the identifying desire in "As I Ebb'd," and one of the primary yearnings that inform the Whitman *oeuvre*, exhibiting a feminine poetics unusual in the nineteenth century.

The "measureless float" is one of Whitman's recurring images, evocative of the maternal in this and other poems as well, and harkening to the hydropathy or water cure movement. The float provides a powerful generative space for Whitman, its amniotic suspension the quintessence of the poet's portrayal of the procreative strengths of the individual and the universe. The float appears, for example, as "the beautiful curious liquid" in one of Whitman's earliest poems, the 1855 "There Was a Child Went Forth." In this poem, Whitman provides a version of the float that incorporates a detailed vignette of the fluid teeming with life: " . . . and the fish suspending themselves so curiously below there . . . and the beautiful curious liquid . . . and the water-plants with their graceful flat heads . . . all became part of him" (Cowley 138). Edwin Havilland Miller observes that the liquid comprises the amniotic fluid, so that in this poem the poet describes his own conception (29). In another 1855 poem, "I Sing the Body Electric," Whitman specifically names this fluid as the "diffused float." He asks, "Do you think matter has cohered together from its diffused float . . . ?" (121). Similarly, in "A Song of the Rolling Earth," Whitman depicts a "fluid vacuum": "The soul's realization and determination still inheriting,/ The fluid vacuum around and ahead still entering and dividing . . ." (67–68). As a further illustration, in an expansive and cosmic section of "Song of Myself," Whitman, with a rhetorical question, asserts his belief in the essential destiny of all energy by positing a "pallid float" as the beginning of life: "If I and you and the worlds and all beneath or upon their surfaces, and all the palpable life, were this moment reduced back to a pallid float, it would not avail in the long run,/ We would surely bring up again where we now stand" (Cowley 79). The pallid float provides a powerful springboard for life on "the worlds and all beneath or upon their surfaces."

Whitman's creation of the image of the float corresponds with hydropathists' conception of water as the spiritual creative essence and medium of the world. As Cayleff describes the water-cure conception, water, "has been used as a curative agent for thousands of years," and is not only a cleansing and purifying agent for the body but for the soul as well. Water has mystical properties, constituting "the primary life-giving substance on earth" (18). Whitman's float parallels the hydropathic reverencing of water, intimating birth and, further, cosmic birth, as the speaker is struck into being from the basic medium of the universe.

Trenchantly, the poet becomes "struck from the float" in a powerful birth image in "Crossing Brooklyn Ferry." The float ends section four of "Crossing Brooklyn Ferry," and the diction of the repeated "I too" mimics the diction of the lines from "As I Ebb'd," quoted above: "I too have bubbled up, floated the measureless float, and been wash'd on your shores." Consider Whitman's similar diction in "Crossing Brooklyn Ferry":

I too had been struck from the float forever held in solution,
I too had receiv'd identity by my body,
That I was I knew was of my body, and what I should be I knew I should be of my
    body. (162)

James Miller has accounted for the float in this way: "The solution appears to be a chemical metaphor for the transcendent liquid in which the divine source-stuff of matter is held diffused and suspended—until the objects and beings of the world are precipitated from it, achieving physical form" (*Walt Whitman's Poetry* 70–71). The lines above have been seen as a germ of the entire poem, and I suggest in addition that they provide a source for Whitman's corpus of poems; the float forever held in solution describes the amniotic state that generates the infant with a body unfolded from the folds, that identifies the semiotic mode from which it will be delivered, eventually into the symbolic. Yet another moment in "Crossing Brooklyn Ferry" designates the float in the climactic final section, in which Whitman conjoins his conception of parturitive space with his conception of what it means to be named:

Throb, baffled and curious brain! throw out questions and answers!
Suspend here and everywhere, eternal float of solution! (164)

Whitman acknowledges the presence of rational discourse that throws out questions and answers, but also affirms the omnipresence of womb space: "Suspend here and everywhere, eternal float of solution!" Surely in that amniotic float await "trillions and trillions" of babes in wombs.

I return now to the sea poems that began my discussion of Whitman's maternal and paternal forces, or *chora* and signifier. In the first of the paired poems, "Out of the Cradle," the bird signifies the speaker: "O you singer solitary, singing by yourself, projecting me" (150). The syntax displays the opposite of what we expect, language the active party, the speaker the one acted upon, so that, unequivocally, the poet becomes constituted by language as the primary mission of that poem. In "As I Ebb'd" the speaker must then contend with the sea who whispered him, and birthed him into the world in which he would then be acted upon by the symbolic. After the crisis of the penultimate section of "As I Ebb'd," in which he tries to suckle from the father and attempts to cross-gender his parents and his relationship with language, and hence his identity within language, he returns to the maternal. In the ultimate section of "As I Ebb'd," no longer attempting to render his father a mother, he works to claim once again the mother's powers, which can no longer lave his entire body nor engulf him, but which he may draw upon.

He begins the last section by comforting the mother, "Ebb, ocean of life, (the flow will return)" (51). He urges her to continue to cry for her castaways, to continue her rustling but not to be so angry. "Cease not," he pacifies her, and recalls her power of moving "endlessly"; he needs her ceaseless rustling in order to prompt the *choric* rhythms that enable his poetry, the maternal repressed that drives his apprehension of the Name-of-the-Father, and he soothes her by saying he meant to treat her "tenderly." With his reclaiming of the mother force he can almost recuperate the *chora*—the recuperation, though, is in the gathering, not the merging—and to this end he perceives the pulsating rhythms vivified in the visual windrows, the "Tufts of straw, sands, fragments." These items, far from disparaging things to claim, indicate the waves of rhythm fundamental to the making of poetry, and they derive from the mother function. The mother function, that comes up "out of the fathomless workings" (65) is the stuff of the body—tear, breath, liquid.

These items are those that the poet does not wish to disclaim but rather to desire, and they are unpretentious things, the visual corollaries of prelingual, gestative pulsions. If rhythms could be seen they would look like these drifts.

I mean tenderly by you and all,
I gather for myself and for this phantom looking down where we lead, and following me and mine.
Me and mine, loose windrows, little corpses,
Froth, snowy white, and bubbles,
(See from my dead lips the ooze exuding at last,
See, the prismatic colors glistening and rolling,)
Tufts of straw, sands, fragments,
Buoy'd hither from many moods, one contradicting another,
From the storm, the long calm, the darkness, the swell,
Musing, pondering, a breath, a briny tear, a dab of liquid or soil,
Up just as much out of fathomless workings fermented and thrown . . . (255–56)

The lines may provide an arresting description of the *chora*, which include the storm of conception followed by the calm, darkness, and swell, and what is born from the fathomless workings of the pulsing prelingual. Whitman humbles the ending, acknowledging the limitations of the symbolic, as well as the frustration of his attempts to return to the *chora*, for the maternal is lost to him in immediate form, except as repressed or partially repressed material. In "Out of the Cradle" the poet remembers his birth into the symbolic realm of language; in "As I Ebb'd," in mid-career as the speaking subject, he recurs to the maternal, accepts his loss, but gathers what he can.

Whitman exits by addressing his readers, reminding them that he and his *choric* yearnings lie at their feet:

We, capricious, brought hither we know not whence, spread out before you,
You up there walking or sitting,
Whoever you are, we too lie in drifts at your feet. (256)

The ending recalls the ending of "Song of Myself" but the triumph remains more quiescent, the merger of subject and object more untrackable, fluid—drifting, if you will. In this way Whitman recurs to a time before language by imaging himself as rhythmic drifts to be perceived by his readers. Almost a century and a-half away from Whitman, we find that if we read him from within his particular language of the maternal and paternal, his speaker almost springs alive in the detritus at our feet even as we find ourselves walking his beach.[12] As he purveys the signifier, he wants to lie at our feet, as one who can almost remember the float and almost desire it enough to turn to it again, finding therein a finale. In the poem's *choric* leanings, suitably victorious for his project of feminine poetics, Whitman acclaims the maternal.

CHAPTER 6

Word, Birth, and Dickinson's Botany Texts

❧❧❧

As a young girl, Emily Dickinson, passionate about the study of botany, compiled her own herbarium, and wrote her friend Abiah Root about the flowers she had collected. Her passion did not abate in adult life, as can be seen by the images taken from botany and used in poems. Flowers and other plants offer a variety of representations in poetry, one of the most pervasive being that of female beauty, an equation *de rigueur* for antebellum American writers. One of the most powerful, though, is that of female eroticism, as seen, for example, in Dickinson's "I tend my flowers for thee—," in which the fuchsia boasts "coral seams," the cactus "splits her Beard," and the roses "break their satin flake—" (Fr367). Indeed, the usage of flowers functions as a kind of language for Dickinson, who often enclosed a bloom in a note to enact exchanges informed by personal but also economic, political, and social concerns.[1] Exchanging flowers was not an uncommon gesture in a culture informed by such books as Frances Sargent Locke Osgood's *The Poetry of Flowers and Flowers of Poetry*, a text even the title of which implies that the natural item and the expression accompanying it are interchangeable.

The two botany texts that Dickinson most likely studied devotedly also promote the idea that flowers express emotional or psychological states. Mrs. Almira H. Lincoln's *Familiar Lectures on Botany* and Alphonso Wood's *A Class-Book of Botany* include such equations of flowers and language in their appendices, Lincoln from her first edition, as early as 1831, and Wood later, in his 1846 edition. For instance, Lincoln, in the section "The Symbolical Language of Flowers," notes that the red columbine signifies that "Hope and fear alternately prevail" (172); the fox-glove that "I am not ambitious for myself, but for you" (172); and the single white pink, "Ingenuousness. Stranger to art" (173). Emily Dickinson may have started with Lincoln's equations, but needless to say found her own as she progressed into her own formulations of language.

The two texts by Lincoln and Wood proved indispensable to Dickinson in her early studies. Jack Capps lists Alphonso Wood's *A Class-Book of Botany* as among those Dickinson was required to study at Mount Holyoke Female Seminary, when she attended in 1847–1848, commencing with it in the junior year, and continuing it in the senior year (189–90). Carlton Lowenberg lists the 1845 edition of Wood as a required text for both Mount Holyoke and Amherst Academy; he points out Wood's emphasis on botany as evidence of God's power, and also Wood's belief in studying more than simply rigid classifications as indicating a holistic approach to biology. Convinced that "nature exemplifies the Creator's purposes and power," Wood also believed that the "natural method," as propounded by Goethe and others, was an attractive alternative to the " 'artificial' method of Linnaeus" (Lowenberg 108–09).

Wood offers almost sensuous descriptions of plants and parts of plants, providing an integrated vocabulary that must have appealed to the Dickinson of "I tend my flowers for thee—" and other such erotic poems. For instance, consider the following description of a kind of trifolium legume: "*Stem* branching, flexuous, suberect; *leaflets* oblong, subentire; *stipules* acuminate; *heads of flowers* loose, roundish; *calyx* hairy, with setaceous teeth. Heads large, deep purple" (II; 118). While hardly prurient reading it, and the countless others like it provide a kind of voluptuous vocabulary unlike that found in most books available to Dickinson.

The other primary text, Almira Lincoln's 1841 and 1845 *Familiar Lectures on Botany,* was used by Dickinson at Amherst Academy, and is noted by Sewall as what may well have been "one of the most important of her school books," containing lessons that proved "a life-giving source" (cited in Lowenberg 70). Among the many science texts that Dickinson used and no doubt valued, including those on physiology, astronomy, anatomy, chemistry, geography, and geology, those on botany seem to speak directly to a poet concerned with language and the feminine. Lincoln's text characterizes the natural world as that which is impervious to the laws of man (13) and seems to laud the discipline of botany as that appropriate particularly to women: "The study of Botany seems peculiarly adapted to females; the objects of its investigation are beautiful and delicate; its pursuits, leading to exercise in the open air, are conducive to health and cheerfulness" (14). Whereas Lincoln frames her discussion in the terms of the cult of true womanhood endemic at the time, she nonetheless opens the door for young women to engage wholeheartedly in the discipline. For example, even as Lincoln meditates upon the native Americans who possessed great knowledge of natural medicines, she seems to envision the search for herbs as enacted by a specifically female Indian (14).

These texts, then, framed at least in part the poet's developing engagement with the natural world, while yet another text provided material specific to Dickinson's region in Massachusetts; published by the junior class of Amherst in 1829, *A Catalogue of Plants Growing Without Cultivation in the Vicinity of Amherst College*, edited by Amherst College President Edward Hitchcock, offered information on local wild plants. Higginson commented on the catalogue, stating that in it "'one can find summer in January,'" a comment Dickinson probably read (Lowenberg 60). Hitchcock's forty students compiled this catalogue as a way to make their botanical studies of the area useful to others, in an enterprising study and publication thereof. So, too, did Dickinson, in her own way, catalogue the area, as Barbara Mallonee suggests: "at fifteen Dickinson had with boundless enthusiasm sought every flower to be found in Amherst, so as she grew older she overstepped the very boundaries of life itself" (238). The *Catalogue of Plants* states of its project that it "'embraces all the indigenous and naturalized plants, that have been discovered and ascertained, within forty or fifty miles of Amherst College'" (cited in Mallonee 232). Dickinson set about to catalogue scrupulously an even smaller area of radius around a different central point—her home.

Concerning Dickinson's own study, I turn expressly to Wood's and Lincoln's presentation of the pod (legume and silique) as a reference point established in the previous chapter, in which I explored Dickinson's use of the image of the pod to negotiate issues of pregnancy. Here I reintroduce that one image to consider the way it appeared in the young Emily Dickinson's textbooks. Each of Wood and Lincoln's texts offer lengthy sections on the subject. Alphonso Wood, for instance, in his exhaustive segment on "Leguminosae," describes the order of beans as important, beautiful, immense, present almost everywhere, redolent, medicinal, and more. Succinctly, he asserts that "no family of the vegetable kingdom possesses a higher claim to the attention of the naturalist than the Leguminosae, whether we regard them as objects of ornament or utility" (II; 110).

Almira Lincoln, in *Familiar Lectures on Botany*, clarifies with her straightforward prose the distinction between legume, silique, and pod, the last subsuming the former two in popular parlance:

LEGUME is a pericarp of two valves, with the seeds attached only to one *suture*, or seam, as the pea. In this circumstance it differs from the silique, which has its seeds affixed to both sutures. The word *pod* is used in common language for both these species of pericarp. (88)

Lincoln's style is more anecdotal than Wood's; for instance, she describes the "Order Decandria—Leguminous Plants" (180) in a way so as to root biology to history—and an exotic history at that. For instance, she claims that "the most savage nations usually pay some attention to Diadelphous plants," ascertaining that Ferdinand de Soto, in Florida before the middle of the sixteenth century, found leguminous seeds among the caches of the natives (180). Probably these were lima beans, she notes, and continue to be cultivated today. Lincoln relies on informal names more than does Wood, itemizing indigo, sandal-wood, liquorice, tamarind, and furze as among the order of legumes. Of the furze, Lincoln relates its beauty: so beautiful is the plant, indeed, that Linnaeus, upon beholding it, "fell upon his knees, in a transport of gratitude, and thanked the Author of nature for thus beautifying the earth" (181). Both Lincoln and Wood use the word "beautiful" liberally in their studies, appearing far from diffident about proclaiming the aesthetic advantages of their discipline, both endorsing botany as evidence of divine involvement in the world.

The two textbook authors provide differing methods of morphologizing, Wood's *A Class-Book of Botany* proving the most throrough. *A Class-Book* exhibits voluminous specific classifications concerning the variations of legumes. Sometimes, for instance, he details the number of joints (from 2–jointed to 6–jointed) (II; 119), as he describes almost lyrically the differing characteristics. The preponderance of words that play variations on the term "oval"—a word that like "ovate" derives from the Latin for "egg"—proves striking in these sections on leguminosae. Many instances of the order of legumes possess characteristics that are oval or ovate, or oblong or oblong-ovate, or ovate-oblong or oval-elliptic, or ovary-like or obovate.[2]

Wood also provides a plethora of terms that suggest erotic associations, as probably virtually any section of a thorough botany book would, given such luxurious terminology—a fact that far from vitiates the point that Dickinson drew her sumptuous lexicon for the female body from botanical studies. Because I have for reasons of streamlining narrowed the range of examples given here to those concerning pods, I give almost exclusively instances that focus on the legume family; in addition to using descriptions that incorporate "ovate" types of words liberally, Wood also describes legumes and siliques in other tantalizing ways. The following constitutes a meager sampler of his suggestive terms: "pod hairy" (II; 111), "transversely bearded" (II; 112), "*pods* pendulous, compressed, rugose" (II; 114), "silky-pubescent" (II; 115), "*fascicles* of flowers ovate" (II; 115), "violet-colored" (II; 116), "egg-shaped" (II; 118), "inflated pods" (II; 125), "turgid pod" (II; 125), "upper lip" (II; 126), and "swelling at the seeds" (II; 126). In one particularly evocative description of a chocolate-producing legume, he relates a stage like a gestative process: "as the pods increase in size, they force themselves into the ground, and there ripen their seeds" (II; 122).

In general, Wood specifies the connection between biology and reproduction in the form of flowers; acknowledging the conflation of beauty, God, aesthetics or taste, science, and parturition, he states in an almost chatty note the following:

To the admirer of nature, flowers are among the first subjects of attention, as mere objects of taste. They are conspicuous for their superior beauty, even in the vegetable kingdom, where all is beautiful. Yet, as objects of science, they merit a still higher regard, whether we consider the Creative skill displayed in their construction, or their important agency in the reproduction of the plant. (I; 28)

Flowers can be appreciated either as important because they are the products of God's skill, or because they are important in the process of reproduction. Interestingly, Wood, at least in regard to his use of syntax above, implies either God or reproduction as equally sufficient to inspire admiration of flowers, putting the natural processes of reproduction on an equal footing with the Christian Deity.

In some ways the language of botany *is* the language of reproduction; Almira Lincoln's *Familiar Lectures on Botany*, too, liberally laces the description of legumes with the vocabulary of parturition. Again, this case is far from unusual in the world of biology, though nonetheless striking for its applications to the poet's project of the feminine body. Lincoln states that the legume contains a placenta and an embryo:

Legume is an irregular, bivalve, elongated pericarp; it is monocephalous, free, the two valves joined by two sutures, an upper and lower; it contains seeds in one cell, a placenta along the lower suture. The embryo has two cotyledons, and a radicle bordering on the hilium. The legume is sabre-form in the bean; cylindric in the Cassia, compound in the pea, and articulated in Hedysarum, where it is called a loment. (90)

Although not particularly stating the primacy of the female function of gestation, Lincoln nonetheless asserts the primacy of nature as a whole over the workings of men when she states, "no systems of man can change the laws and operations of Nature" (13). Almira Lincoln's text, along with Alphonso

Wood's, evidences an equaling of God and reproduction that, in its subtle way, implies that parturition forms a reason in itself to admire the workings of life—and one can perceive such a process as a system of operations as more reliable than the laws of man, in Lincoln's case, and equal to the workings of God, in Wood's case.

In her poetry, Emily Dickinson evinces this dichotomizing of systems: nature as versus either man or God. Her poems are aware of the desire to at least equalize the feminine workings of nature with the systems of man in the one case, or the workings of God in the other; she desires, that is, for the feminine to equal or exceed. The ascendancy of nature over man and perhaps God that is intimated in her textbooks, Wood's *A Class-Book of Botany* and Lincoln's *Familiar Lectures on Botany*, becomes a primacy in which Dickinson in turn invests her conception of language. This conception of language is maternally invested, and draws at least in part from Dickinson's poems of nature, because through the usage of botanical and other nature images she can attempt to find her own means of expression that does not need to be filtered through patriarchal naming but can stand on its own as erotic female expression.

The woman poet must discover her own liturgies, finding a feminine naming that avoids the diminishment of the female body. In Dickinson's *oeuvre* we can see a startling usage of a kind of language that distinguishes itself from the patronymic, or that which depends upon the phallic signifier. Dickinson works toward a kind of matronymic language early on, in one of her poems of juvenilia. The early poem resolves with these irreverent, and playful, three lines:

In the name of the Bee—
And of the Butterfly—
And of the Breeze—Amen! (Fr23)

Of course the bee and butterfly and breeze are anonymous—they need no surname at all—in stark contrast to the Name-of-the-Father, which *is* surname. The listing of natural elements could be seen as a kind of Transcendental gesture, and certainly some of the flavor of the Transcendental pertains, but Dickinson's utilization of nature goes further than that. The attraction of bee and butterfly and breeze for Dickinson's project of female expression depends primarily upon the fact of their anonymity; the namelessness that they offer to Dickinson prompts new options for a language that is not patriarchal language. Similarly, the trinity invoked several lines above in the same fascicle (what used to be considered, according to Johnson, the same poem), "Summer—Sister—Seraph!" (Fr22), skirts naming and opens up the intimation of a site beyond that of the proper name. As she hints at the matronymic, Dickinson takes the Name-of-the-Father in vain.

What confounds the imagination is that Dickinson understood a century and a half ago the problems central to a woman writing in patriarchal language: having to negotiate meaning, and meaninglessness, in a world *a priori* male, needing to use female language, and finding the task of trying to create it a vexed one. An astonishing perspicacity informs the poems of matronymic expression, a suffusion of purpose that announces her awareness of the final nonutility of the signifier. Moreover, the poems find a joy unparalleled in the collection of Emily Dickinson's work.

I investigate further the poet's matronymic language in the final section of this chapter; I wish, however, to enter first into an extended discussion of her God-invested language, so as to provide a background for the dilemma of patriarchal language, before presenting the alternative of feminine language. I examine here first the ways in which Dickinson discovers the inadequacies of that patriarchal system of naming for her artistic purposes; toward that goal I return to Fascicle Twenty-Eight, the poems therein providing an excellent workshop by which to show Dickinson's inherited conception of language that relies upon the Puritan belief in God as the positor of meaning. Such a conception of language necessitates a belief in a signifier and signified matching directly to make a conventional system of correspondences, a conception of language from which the poet will ultimately abdicate in order to embrace matrilineal expression. I wish to show here the progression of her abdication, for within such progress is contained Dickinson's acute critique of language itself.

If Dickinson must undo the word before she can exist as a writer of maternal expression, she must first understand how that word works. The name, in particular the proper name or surname, aggravates an awareness for women in regard to their positioning within patronymic culture, as Denise Riley suggests in equating Sojourner Truth's famous refrain, "Ain't I a woman?" with the plea, "'Ain't I a fluctuating identity?" (1). In other words, to be a woman in patriarchal culture is to experience oneself as unsettled and vicissitudinous, and the workings of the patriarchal name apprehended by Dickinson in her poetry can serve to adjudicate such uncertainties as a woman attempts to discover female identity. Accordingly0, I observe Dickinson's struggle with the behavior of the signifier, both patriarchal and Puritan, before I return to her discovery of the anonymous feminine. She must grapple with the ultimate signified for "God," debunking the signifier by taking God's name in vain. Toward this end I will focus on the opening and closing poems of Fascicle Twenty-Eight, which interrogate the nature of signification by calling specifically upon the activity of prayer as a language activity with its own inherent commitments to the signified.

In Fascicle Twenty-Eight Emily Dickinson grapples with conventional theories of language as she contends with the nature of prayer, because it offers the possibility of God as the conventional authenticator of the signifier. Dickinson's relationship with words devolves from the Puritan tradition, in which speakers "made the relationships between Word and flesh, words and deeds, central tenets of their faith" (Kamensky 5). The Puritans assumed that "in the order of the universe the connection between words and the things they signify is a God-ordained, immutable one" (Grabo 57). In previous centuries, theories of language afforded the hope that ultimate meaning is endorsed by the Deity, and Dickinson lingers at that hope before she explodes it. For Dickinson the condition of prayer appoints a trust in the promise that a collection of signifiers can find exact corollaries in signifieds, with no slippage; the naming involved in prayer might describe a kind of utopian language, if only it would prove its correspondences.

The organization of Fascicle Twenty-Eight tracks exactly how a God-invested language could be dislodged. Puritan understandings of language involved experiencing all earthly occurrences as signifiers for heavenly signifieds, a tradition that presents a faith in the unification of language and meaning, of fortuitous correspondence that occurs in the process of saying. Dickinson had to work in the wake of this tradition, and find her own way, as we see her doing when she considers prayer as a form of saying. Prominent to Fascicle Twenty-Eight are the first and last, bookended, poems, both of which register dissatisfaction with the commitments of prayer as signification. Sharon Cameron suggests that the first and last poems of many fascicles are relational—complementary or oppositional, or both (*Choosing* 34). Oberhaus, too, in working with Fascicle Forty, posits the fascicle's "envelope structure" (22), in that the last two poems mirror the first two; the beginning and ending poems prove chiastic.[3] The bracketing poems in Fascicle Twenty-Eight complement each other in describing the speaker's relationship with the signifier that is authorized by God.

Dickinson considers signification in Fascicle Twenty-Eight through the experience of prayer, which is highlighted in the bracketing poems. In the opening poem, "My period had come" (Fr525), Dickinson begins by considering her relationship with God through prayer, whereas in the closing poem, "I prayed, at first, a little" (Fr546), she comes to jettison God in favor of the verity of her own emotions. In the first poem the speaker announces that she has come to consider prayer as a particular kind of aesthetic system: "My period had come/ for Prayer—/ No other Art—would do—"; the presence of God is uncertain from the beginning, however, as the speaker must ask, "Creator—Was it you?"

If one espouses a view of correspondences derived from Puritan ideas of language, then the assurance of God's presence is a must. God must hold down the meanings without the certainty that He exists—the proof of the signifier's signified—the word's referent—then the act of speech remains without grounding, and communication is necessarily gibberish. Dickinson makes sure that we understand that her topic is the "sign," a particularly trenchant word, as it indicates the yearning for language as a system of signs, but also allows the "sign" as revelatory experience. To look for a sign is to ensconce oneself within the Puritan tradition that understands every earthly signifier to have been provided with an exact signified, and such correspondence the heavenly Father would protect. What occurs in this opening poem, however, is that no sign is given.

The speaker cannot find the house of God, and her experience becomes frightening as she finds no house and no sign:

His House was not—No sign
had He—
By Chimney nor by Door
Could I infer his Residence—
+Vast Prairies of Air

Unbroken by a Settler—
Were all that I could see—
Infinitude—Hads't Thou no
Face
That I might look on thee?

What we see developing in this poem is chilling[4]: the speaker, perhaps a girl who is learning to pray, begins to use language in order to find meaning which, the devout might hope, would exist in heaven. What she finds, however, is nothing; the "sign" she wants, the idea of language as anchored in God, does not appear in the poem, and she finds instead the lack of a sign. In a universe that ascends horizons and discovers vastness, she realizes she can find no ingress. In fact, the poem stands as remarkable for its negations: no, missed, not, no, nor, un-, no, not, which establish a negative currency that militates against the hope for congruency in signification. Furthermore, the fascicle rendering of the poem, as presented above, emphasizes the word "Face," accorded a line to itself and rendered more poignant for the fact that the line before it clarifies that the face may not exist. The possible facelessness of God thus becomes accentuated because of this line positioning, the quandary of one praying to an absence displayed in all its disheartening force. The word of God can no longer be a sign in the sense of omen, and it cannot operate as an exact equation of word and meaning, given the absences in this poem.

Another poem, not in Fascicle Twenty-Eight, helps elucidate the fascicle poem by summarizing this existential nature of prayer:

Prayer is the little implement
Through which Men reach
Where Presence—is denied them.
They fling their Speech

By means of it—in God's Ear—
If then He hear—
This sums the Apparatus
Comprised in Prayer—(Fr623)

In this poem, too, the presence of a signified is in question. Men fling their speech, but this God may exist but simply be indifferent, or deaf, or intermittently deaf. The essential "if" condition of this God's ability to hear renders the poem without resolution, prayer remaining simply apparatus and not meaningful interaction. The God in the first fascicle poem, "My period had come," though, may well resist meaning to the point of the speaker's questioning whether God exists at all. The speaker finds no way to infer his residence, only air and infinitude where his house might be.

Indeed, within such lack of meaning silence gains importance, and to this effect, David Porter comments that the speaker of "My period had come" searches for, "then opens upon a great silent space of incomprehension" (161).[5] Interestingly, God has no character—he cannot be inferred nor can his face be seen, though in the final stanza, silence is almost a character:

The Silence condescended—
+Creation stopped—for Me—
But awed beyond my Errand
I worshiped—did not "pray"—
  +stood—+Reach—touch—
  +Wide Prairies + The Heavens paused—

The speaker at the end of "My period had come" doesn't pray, an act involving words. Instead, words fail her, and the only course of action left, presumably, is that of revering the silence. Eberwein, too, sees the ending as a failure of language: "the speaker found herself unable to mouth the formulas of prayer or even to assure herself of an audience" after "having failed to articulate religious language" (258). Whether we understand the ending of the opening poem as a triumphant experience of awe or a failure to communicate with God, we must weigh the impact of the silence as an impediment to contact.

Dickinson's dictionary offers several perspectives on the word "pray." Webster ascertains that "pray" "belongs to the same family as *preach* and *reproach*," an insight cogent to the irony of this poem, in which prayer is an implied reproach to an absent or nonexistent God. To pray is "1. To ask . . . " and "2. To petition . . . ," both activities imbued with a hope that language might offer a means to verify the equation between signifier and signified. The third definition stipulates that to pray is "In *worship*, to address the Supreme Being . . ." and it is fitting that the speaker of the fascicle poem ends with worshiping. This third definition proffers also a quotation from scripture: "When thou *prayest*, enter into thy closet, and when thou hast shut the door, *pray* to thy Father who is in secret, and thy Father who seeth in secret, shall reward thee openly. Matt vi." The scriptural addition to the definition piques an interest in the importance of secrecy to Dickinson, the poet with utmost respect for the division between private and public, prayer and open worship.[6] It also underscores the fact that there is no open reward in the poem.

The ending of the initial poem of Fascicle Twenty-Eight may be uneasy, but the ending of the closing poem brings unmitigated uncertainty. This poem, "I prayed, at first, a little" (Fr546), also starts with a young speaker attempting to believe in signifiers:

I prayed, at first, a little
Girl,
Because they told me to—
But stopped, when qualified
to guess
How prayer would+ feel—to me—

The conventional teachers, the "they" who tell the girl how to pray, might have instructed her that congruency comes with the language of prayer, and she trusts at first that prayer might bring results, but ceases to trust when she tests prayer against her own emotions. The fascicle version singles out the word "Girl," and presents it in a line to itself, emphasizing both her gender and her aloneness in pursuing the weighty question of prayer.[7] Very quickly the young speaker is thrown back on her own resources, and uses as her authority not God but her own feelings.[8] She tests prayer with the litmus of her emotions: "How prayer would feel—to me—."

The last two stanzas of "I prayed, at first, a little," emphasize the uncertainty of the enterprise of prayer as signification. At first the reader wonders if the poem might end in equilibrium because of the strong God the speaker invokes, but the poem upends such possible expectations and refuses closure:

And often since, in Danger,
I count the force 'twould
be
To have a God so strong
As that
To hold +my life for me

Till I could +take the Balance
That+ tips so frequent, now,
It takes me all the while
to poise—
+And then—it doesn't stay—
 +sound + supposed +solemn—
+under—further + the light +
Catch my + slips so easy +
It is not steady—tho'—

_____

It is impossible in print to reproduce the graphics of the fascicle: in the manuscripts the line drawn at the end of this poem is broken and unsteady, a mark commensurate with the unsteadiness of the poem. As with "My period had come," this poem offers word variants that appear almost to form their own stanza, a kind of echoing stanza after the final stanza, its fragmentation offering a lyric in and of itself, a disrupted coda or postscript.[9]

Dickinson suspends the reader in the gathering of forces that the single line "to poise" offers, before the poem fractures expectations with the last line. The speaker is poised only to be thrown off balance again, so that hope forms only to blast the thought of hope, so that nothing in this type of signification remains in accordance with balance or congruency or equivalency. Signification is off kilter; God proves weak or nonexistent; prayer cannot test verity (though perhaps emotion can).

Just two fascicle pages before "I prayed, at first, a little," Dickinson presents another discursis on the meaning of verbal exchange in the poem, "'Heaven' has different" (Fr544), which threads the bookended poems together in that it likewise discusses language. Like the first poem it questions the nature of the sign, and like the last it ends in uncertainty. The placing of "Heaven" in quotation marks directly questions the nature of the signifier, wherein Dickinson suggests that although Christianity might encourage a balanced ratio of signifier to signified, she intuits different signs, different possibilities:

116

"Heaven" has different
Signs—to me—
Sometimes, I think that Noon
Is but a symbol of the Place—

The poem tantalizes with the hint of equivalency, for noon might be a symbol for heaven, but the poem only hints at the equivalency by stipulating the "Sometimes," and then continues to describe what men might call "Paradise" to end up lamenting in this slippery poem that we cannot yet tell what the signified is: "Not yet, our eyes can see—." A slippery poem lodged in between two slippery poems at the furthest reaches of Fascicle Twenty-Eight: here the word of God is not the word of God, because he may well not exist. That leaves us on our own with language, and if that is so, we have a topsy-turvy affair. Dickinson's relationship with Puritanism in these poems imbeds prayer as a sort of received language theory for Emily Dickinson, and one against which she must militate, for the nature of signification, a poignant and sometimes frightening topic for her, resists, in the end, the notion of prayer as equation.

Finally, another poem in the middle of Fascicle Twenty-Eight continues the presentation of vexed signification, the course of the fascicle offering a sort of practicum on the signifying that Dickinson must negotiate, given the absence of the locked signifier–signified equation that Christianity promises. One of the types of signifying she identifies, "reckoning," targets the falsely promised signification of heaven. Reckoning includes judgment as in the day of reckoning, reckoning as surmise, and reckoning that is tabulation. The most famous instance of reckoning in Fascicle Twenty-Eight, the poem "I reckon—when I count" (Fr533), proffers such a saturated sense of variations on reckoning:

I reckon—when I count
at all—
First—Poets—Then the Sun—
Then Summer—Then the
Heaven of God—
And then—the List is done—

But, looking back—the
First so seems
To comprehend the Whole—
The Others look a needless Show—
So I write—Poets—All—

Their Summer—lasts a solid
Year—
They can afford a Sun
The East—would deem
Extravagant—
And if the +Further Heaven—

Be Beautiful As they +prepare
+For Those who +worship Them—
It is too difficult a Grace—
To justify the Dream—

+Other—final + Disclose +to
+Trust in +Ask of—

The kind of scrutiny Dickinson brings here to the "Heaven of God," especially heaven as it might provide the hope for meaning in language, is one already located in the bracketing poems of Fascicle Twenty-Eight. The heaven of God constitutes a "Further Heaven," more distant than one might be able to reach, and more difficult. As in the first and last poems of the fascicle, Dickinson subtends a heaven more diversionary than ultimate, more bluster than reward, lacking the correspondence or meaning to reward the word—in some way unaccountable. Wolosky notes cogently in "I reckon—when I count" that "the interest in language for its own sake is a function of lost proximity to the divine" (153–54); just so, in the last two lines we find a formulation that restates the loss: "It is too difficult a Grace—/ To justify the Dream."

Dickinson sets up the worth of God-invested language against the language of poets and she opts, interestingly and irreverently, for the language of poets that can "comprehend" the whole, including the "Heaven of God." Poets comprehend—they both understand and, in understanding, subsume—and in this way the list really is "done"—that is, both finished and worked. The word "list" carries overtones, as it might recall the "list" of the saved that Calvinism promotes and that Dickinson personally had to endure as a schoolgirl when Mary Lyon presented a list of the young schoolmates who were saved.[10] In this poem the list records the first (poets) becoming the comprehensive (the whole) of the list, the primary the everything, and one need not, finally, count at all: one need only say "poets."[11]

In "I reckon—when I count" Dickinson prominently mentions summer as ally to the poet. In several of her most feminine poems of artistic primacy, she martials the forces of nature to grant herself the authority to challenge patriarchal language. Emily Dickinson, ultimately, does not want to name names; she wants to unname them, thereby producing iconoclastic poetry that challenges the Name-of-the-Father. Any poet must question the assumption of meaning that naming bears, the way words presume to fasten meaning, and doubly so must a woman poet, crucially and mortally, come to grips with the snares of the signifier. Dickinson's poems of the Name-of-the-Father are always at the least uneasy and, at the most, passionately denunciatory, so that her attitudes toward naming demonstrate belief that is undone by wrenching disbelief. In contradistinction to patriarchal naming (God, father, husband), which insists upon a discrepancy in power and involves naming at the expense of the female body, her feminine expression often brings an elation for the female speaker.[12] By needs paradoxical, the namelessness of female naming—a "sumptuous Destitution"—descries an ecstasy, a moment that goes unrecorded, a secular miracle, usually small.

Central to poems of Dickinson's matronymic language, "Sweet Mountains—Ye tell Me no lie—" (Fr745) turns what is usually a phallic landscape into a female one.[13] Prominently in this poem, the speaker shows her capacity to "take the Royal names in vain—," and indeed, takes the name of the father in vain, and so finds a female way of worship distinct from prayer directed to the Father:

Sweet Mountains—Ye tell Me no lie—
Never deny Me—Never fly—
Those same unvarying Eyes
Turn on Me—when I fail—or feign,
Or take the Royal names in vain—
Their far—slow—Violet Gaze—

The mountains' style of telling seems to be a way of looking which proves incapable of lies, and comforts the speaker; it constitutes exactly what it is, with no slippage. She can take the royal names in vain, but nothing disastrous ensues, and instead steadiness prevails, because of the femaleness of this mode that, with its language of looking, heralds nonslippage.

Especially in the second stanza, the poem proves remarkable for its burgeoning female images:

My strong Madonnas—Cherish still—
The Wayward Nun—beneath the Hill—
Whose service—is to You—
Her latest Worship—When the Day
Fades from the Firmament away—
To lift Her Brows on You—(Fr745)

She worships best as day fades and night, the province of the feminine, approaches. Not only does the day recede but attention to the firmament (the place of God) segues to attention on what is beneath the hill, in the earth. Interestingly, the poem gives not one Madonna, but plural Madonnas, a world of mothers who will safeguard their novitiate, enfolded in the hill, the womb of the earth. In an odd and wonderful adumbration, the lift of her brows at the end of the poem mirrors the ridgeline of the mountains.

Often Dickinson uses nature poems to supplant the patronym, as, for example, with the butterfly "That doesn't know its Name" (Fr1559), in which the act of being anonymous highlights the freedom of living beneath, or beyond, the aegis of signification. As in her poem of juvenilia, "In the name of the Bee—," Dickinson shows denizens of nature existing in a nameless state, living their lives outside the bounds of man-made language. Dickinson accordingly reveres them, finding joy in their exemplary status, and identifying with their kind of nonstatus, except that her nonstatus as a woman comes from within the defiles of the signifier, and the animal's from without. Namelessness can be respite from blame, for in "Bloom upon the mountain stated" (Fr787), Dickinson extemporizes in the next line that the bloom is "Blameless of a Name—." Other poems, too, feature namelessness: the "nameless Bird—" (Fr1109); the sea's "nameless Fathoms" (Fr1175), both of which rely upon feminine nightscapes; and "A Vastness" that comes "without Face, or Name" (Fr1104) as twilight progresses. The denizens of nature and the images of night together summon a freeing namelessness and femininity.

The most essential avatar of the nameless multitudes of nature, though, arrives in the form of an entire season—and that season for Dickinson remains, ineluctably, summer. Having already explored in chapter three the feminine themes in the summer poem, "My first well Day—since," we turn to other poems here (Fr288). A poem describing a weed of summer distills the multitudinous themes of summer for Dickinson that include femininity, nature, infamy or anonymity, and joy; the "Weed of Summer" stands without name because she does not know her "station low/ Nor Ignominy's Name—/ Bestowed a summer long/ Upon a fameless flower—/ Then swept as lightly from disdain/ As Lady from her Bower—" (Fr1617). This poem finds a standard nineteenth-century equivalency between flowers and women, and uses it to emphasize the condition of low station, ignominy, namelessness, famelessness, and a bowered existence, but more than that the poem discovers a bliss that remains an important component of Dickinson's feminine, nameless summer. On another occasion of naming, the bees "thought the Summer's name/ Some rumor of Delirium" (Fr361); the notion that summer's name might, instead of existing as signifier, inhere in an altered state, delirium, goes far to describe what kind of language Dickinson attempts to discover and use. In "How know it from a Summer's Day?" (Fr1412) Dickinson similarly describes "Fervors" and that which "scintillates" in the birds and the bees who are "Vans without a name."[14]

Summer represents the ecstatic possibilities posed by delirium and fervors, and made practicable by namelessness. In poem after poem about summer Dickinson captures an ecstasy in feminine naming, as in the poem, "The last of Summer is Delight—" (Fr1380), which claims it an audacious undertaking "To meet it [Summer]—nameless as it is—." Well might it be audacious to meet a nameless thing, for in such a meeting one meets a thing that is uncontrollable. Dickinson tries to describe states of fevered joy so uncontrollable that one may not label or report them; they are, specifically, "In many and reportless places" (Fr1404).

Occasions of reportless joy speak directly to the point; one may not report them because they are not susceptible to the signifier, and hence exist in a languageless realm:

In many and reportless places
We feel a Joy—
Reportless, also, but sincere as Nature
Or Deity—

It comes, without a consternation—
Dissolves—the same—
But leaves a sumptuous Destitution—
Without a Name—

Sumptuous destitution without a name: the oxymoron imports the moment as sumptuous and blissful (Dickinson offers "blissful" as a word variant for "sumptuous"), even though penurious. The destitution may indicate a world impoverished because of the cultural disregard for the feminine, but blissful as a result, knowing no boundaries, not even the ones imposed by the signifier. The moment comes, erotically, and nothing about it can be solved, but only dissolved. Clearly Dickinson offers a matronymic alternative here, a moment beyond the patronymic, a *jouissance* intense exactly because of its feminine possibilities.

Another poem begins with the murmuring of bees that gives way to some "Posterior, prophetic" murmuring (Fr1142), perhaps not unlike the *chora* that exists as a site before language. The denizens of nature in this poem are sent by "The Typic Mother" (Fr1142), the fact of whom exists as alternative to the problematic existence of God, thereby accentuating Dickinson's creation of a female world. In the world of Puritan language, God is positioned in order to realize the signifieds, so that signification can have meaning, and thus that Name-of-the-Father prevails. In the world presided over by the Typic Mother, anonymity prevails; because the "Genesis was June," the first book of the Bible changes from Genesis to the ecstatic Dickinsonian world of summer, June. The world moves not from word to word, but "As Accent fades to interval," a maternal mode finding anonymity in *choric* nuances of accent and interval. The poem locates a timelessness caught between speculation about the future and realization of the past: "Till what we could not see, has been" (Fr1142). Aptly, one of the variants for that line reads, "Till what we could not name has been." Mysterious, joyous, revelatory, what has been has existed without a name, and has existed without a name by grace of the Typic Mother, who offers an alternative to the conventional correspondences of patriarchal language.

Dickinson intimates the existence of a mode in which the signifier does not work, exploring a needlessness to naming, showing that once naming is withheld, man-made (patriarchally constructed) boundaries explode into a *jouissance* attendant upon anonymity, the lack of the signifier. Interestingly, these nameless denizens may indicate not only flowers and other natural elements, but women as they must survive, beneath notice, in society. With a kind of apophradic vision,[15] we can look back from Ralph Ellison's evocation of minority existence in *Invisible Man* and see Dickinson's nameless women. In Ellison's novel an entire sector of society exists off the timeline of history, not visible to mainstream culture, as in Dickinson's poems a culture of women exists nameless to history, invisible, beneath renown.

In the aforementioned poem, "Bloom upon the Mountain—stated—" (Fr787), in which the bloom is "Blameless of a Name—," the bloom's relation to society carries such a sense of invisibility:

Who for tilling—to the Mountain
Come, and disappear—
Whose be Her Renown, or fading,
Witness, is not here—

She comes and disappears—and no one witnesses her coming and disappearing, her renown or her fading; like Ellison's people she remains invisible to the powers-that-be, and her actions, beneath history and beneath notice, are of no consequence to them. Keeping "Recordless Company—," consorting with those who "have no Robes, nor Names—" (Fr303), she forges beyond the signifier. In "The Sun went down—no Man looked on—" (Fr1109), twice the speaker tells us that "no Man" is watching, while "A nameless Bird—a Stranger/ Were Witness for the Crown—." Something momentous can happen even if not recorded by the patriarchy—perhaps, especially if not recorded by any name; indeed, the bird's namelessness seems to enable her to accomplish her extraordinary activity. In a related poem, pictures that "No Man drew" are posited while "People" "of Gossamer—/ And Eider—names—" (Fr577) go about their business. Again, a culture of anonymous people with eider names that men do not record in history or in pictures exists almost parallel to the world of men.[16] This anonymous, feminine culture, of "station low" and "Ignominy's Name" (Fr1617), as mentioned above, inhabits a world that indubitably exists: "Their names, unless you know them,/ 'Twere useless tell./ Of bumble-bees and other nations/ The grass is full" (Fr1764). Not only one nation but many nations thrive here, though it is useless to tell the names because they are untellable in patriarchal language.

A world of women does exist in Dickinson, and a couple intriguing poems carry the notion even further, as for instance, in one brief poem, "The Robin for the Crumb/ Returns no syllable/ But long records the Lady's name/ In Silver Chronicle" (Fr810). Here the woman is anonymous, but gloriously so, because she is sung by the nonlingual bird who praises the lady's kindness in giving up a crumb. The lady's name, strictly speaking, is bird song. In another poem, about two women, "Precious to Me—She still shall be—" (Fr751), Dickinson follows this first line with the line, "Though She forget the name I bear—." In this relationship, the names of the two women prove unimportant as long as their remembrance of each other instead depends upon the "Summer's Everlasting Dower—" (Fr751) that they share.

Dickinson constructs the world of namelessness tentatively in a letter to Susan Gilbert Dickinson, in some ways a typical love letter that asserts with urgency that only the two lovers can understand each other. At the same time, however, this passionate letter decries language, declaring that bodily presence is enough and that given the gift of presence the two women would not ask for language. Words fail Dickinson in this letter because, as she sees it, they are irrelevant:

Susie, forgive me Darling, for every word I say—my heart is full of you, none other than you in my thoughts, yet when I seek to say to you something not for the world, words fail me. If you were here—and Oh that you were, my Susie, we need not talk at all, our eyes would whisper for us, and your hand fast in mine, we would not ask for language . . . (L94)

If there exists a way to tell that defies the signifier, then that way is the language of nature, the way of the body. Dickinson tries to communicate things that are not for the world in the ways that the world usually constructs meaning and, not surprisingly, she feels that words prove inept to the task. The signifier ties her to patriarchal culture as pinned by the signifier, and the two women of the above letter have things to tell that are untellable within the strictures of that culture. Hence, words fail them; what does not fail, however, is the body, the eyes and hands that make it so that they do not need to ask for language.

One final poem, serving to encapsulate what I have been calling the matronymic, heralds the "Seraphic May" and in so doing suggests a world of feminine possibility in the word "May." The poem operates as a kind of female *carpe diem* that might overturn Herrick, the darling rosebuds of May being given the active part. Women keep their "recordless company with women, and revel in anonymity, their dance summoning the pulsions of the *chora* which redetermine the drives and rhythms of poetry as it might be written by a woman:

There is a morn by men unseen—
Whose maids upon remoter green
Keep their Seraphic May—
And all day long, with dance and game,
And gambol I may never name—
Employ their holiday.

Here to light measure, move the feet
Which walk no more the village street—
Nor by the wood are found—
Here are the birds that sought the sun
When last year's distaff idle hung
And summer's brows were bound.

Ne'er saw I such a wondrous scene—
Ne'er such a ring on such a green—
Nor so serene array—
As if the stars some summer night
Should swing their cups of Chrysolite—
And revel till the day—

Like thee to dance—like thee to sing—
People upon the mystic green—
I ask, each new May Morn.
I wait thy far, fantastic bells—
Announcing me in other dells—
Unto the different dawn! (Fr13)

Herein Dickinson records a vision that wanders within and beyond the dictates of Mrs. Almira Lincoln's *Familiar Lectures on Botany*, wherein Lincoln espoused the study of botany for women especially. Dickinson's botanical studies have taken her far afield from Lincoln's textbook to a utopic possibility of female expression, particularly viewed through the beauties of nature. The mystic people, unseen by men, find their own "holiday," or holy day, and claim it for their own; theirs is a gambol, importantly, that the speaker "may never name." Of no renown, they provide their own company on the "remoter green," and find a "light measure" to "move the feet," inaugurating a measure that will serve for feminine song. In speaking of female writing, Toril Moi explains that Hélène Cixous finds a kind of woman's writing as forming in a time before Oedipal concerns: Cixous "presents this nameless pre-Oedipal space filled with mother's milk and honey as the sources of the song that resonates through all female writing" (114). Dickinson may be intuiting precisely such a nameless, preoedipal space of mother's milk and honey.

The line, "And gambol I may never name—," resonates memorably because naming from such a preoedipal place proves impossible, it being the nature of maids in May, the existence of the dance, and the feminine "light measure." The gambol may never be named because the maids keep recordless company, finding their voice in the measure that comes before voice, and so keep record beyond the telling of it. Presumably last year the distaff hung idle and summer was bound—but now summer is free and the scene wondrous. The women swing cups, female images, in a scene that knows no other bounds than that of song and the body language of dance. In the dawn following the night's revels, the speaker is finally announced, not by her surname or by any particular signifier, but by "fantastic bells" that respect her anonymity in this world and instead announce her in "other dells," yet another female image, and a place where language is not needed. In a different dawn indeed, beyond the Name-of-the-Father, women dance in gambols they "may never name," discovering their anonymous yet powerful way to say.

Conclusion: Reading Poetry from One Century to Another

"I had not thought, until this hour
When passing from the earth, that ear
Of any, were it not the shade
Of one whom in life I made
All mystery but a simple name,
Might know the secret of a spirit . . ."

"What is it then between us?
What is the count of the scores or hundreds of years between us?"

"To Being, somewhere—Motion—Breath—
Though Centuries beyond,
And every limit a Decade—
I'll shiver, satisfied."

Edgar Allan Poe, Walt Whitman, and Emily Dickinson lean to the mode of namelessness, beyond the word, and such leaning identifies an important posture in their attitude toward expression. They rapture language so that in our reading we can experience, with them, signification on the edge, signification that desires moving beyond itself. Celebrating or coopting the female body, especially the body of the mother, they find a mode wherein language glides, or dissolves, discovering *choric* intensity that suggests rhythms not of the patriarchal mode of signification. Through their discovery of a *jouissance* that defies the Name-of-the-Father, they experiment with language at the edge, where signification crumbles, playing around the brink of the real. Their poetries vivify the American poetries to come in the following century and beyond. Usage of the feminine mode complicates signification, already slipping, always off-balance and in danger. Poe, Whitman, and Dickinson want continually to move in the direction of namelessness. These poets influence United States poetry in the ways that they use feminine uttterance.

I have concentrated on the significatory characteristics of the three poets, on their awareness of liminal sexualities that enable them to be desiring subjects by means of demanding more of language than it can sometimes give. Homosexuality, refusal to marry, consideration of the status of the unborn, consciousness after death: they grapple with the representation of nonconformist forms of sexuality, or that which is taboo or repressed or unmentionable. These sexualities were culturally inadmissible in the nineteenth century, and in acknowledging them, Poe, Whitman, and Dickinson push the boundaries of language, demonstrating their interest in balancing on the edge of what is signifiable, and forcing that envelope. They know there exist things that may not be said—that not only may not be said but can not, are impossible to say—and they yearn toward the fringe of that void. If language is desire what is the desire for childbirth that precludes language? How does one say the longings of homosexuality in a culture that lacks the contemporaneous signification to define homosexuality as a culture? What is consciousness of desire beyond death?[1]

The poets operate, in their most memorable moments, on the precipice of language, at the Lacanian *barre*, on the cliff of the sayable overarching the unknown or the unsayable. Were they aware of the enormous shifts in language their sexually marginalized poetries might cause? The evidence of their awareness arises in the posings and supposings in which they engage with their readers; they wink at us, realizing intimacies that change over time as each poet engages with successive generations of readers and points to the existence of poetry that is aware of such engagements with the reader.

Such self-aware poetry takes into scope the changing relationship with language that each new generation of readers might have. Poe, Whitman, and Dickinson evince an intensive awareness of audience and the shifting capabilities of that audience to play along with projects that go beyond naming. It may seem paradoxical to say that their relationship with various eras of readers depends upon the relationship of their poetry to the body, for one might think that disembodiment would operate as the precondition to a legacy of future readers, but just the opposite is the case. Expressly because the poet has a body may his or her writing be rediscovered in each generation. In touching the body we might take the hint, the wink, and apprehend the mode beyond the signifier. More correct than saying that every generation renews the poetries of this triad of poets would be to say that their poetries birth readers in successive futures, so that the reader discovers Poe, Whitman, and Dickinson anew to the extent that the reader is able to apprehend the body. Their poems encode an understanding of the need to wait, possibly decades or centuries, for the reader who can touch them, as the poems touch and startle us.

In talking of the project of poetry and the body, Robert McClure Smith states that, "most obviously, the insistence on a transformative equation between 'body' and 'text' is equally fundamental [to Emily Dickinson as] to the poetic project of Walt Whitman" (129). He sees both Whitman and Dickinson, as do I, engaged in a kind of proto-version of *écriture féminine*, a writing of the body as text. Poe, too, writes the body as text in a more limited way. As Renza points out, "someone like Poe was convinced that a writer's very autograph and handwritten manuscript could express his 'moral biography'" (64). Poe anticipates the Whitmanian kind of urge to give the reader his hand, his body, in order to have him altogether, and Dickinson wishes to register her poetry on the pulse, her verse on the nerves and veins.

Dickinson points out that, "A Word made Flesh is seldom/ And tremblingly partook/ Nor then perhaps reported . . ." (Fr1715). Even though the body of the text may seldom find readers to partake of it, as of a communion, still the few readers such a bodily text affects are touched powerfully, so that they tremble. Such a text, rare and crucial, may be fashioned so as to let off its power over time, for successive generations, affecting each reader according to that reader's capacity to register the reading; such a text is gauged "To our specific strength—" (Fr1715). The poem acknowledges the "consent of Language," so that language exists here as a being in itself that can grant consent; this language has the power to grant consent to its future readers, too.

Whitman demonstrates a similar vigilance about understanding language that moves his readers, fully aware as he is that language starts before and ends after any single human being; it makes him as he goes, and can continue making after he expires. Like Dickinson, Whitman realizes his strategy, too, through the body as text. Most famously, Whitman asks for us to look for him beneath our bootsoles at the end of "Song of Myself," a clear reference to himself as a corporeal being who exists in the material world, and whom we reference in our reading, and who references us. Even more powerfully than the ending of "Song of Myself" does the ending of "The Sleepers" designate a sort of time-released reader: "Not the womb yields the babe in its time more surely than I shall be yielded from you in my time" (204). By "my time" Whitman may mean not the time of his historical era, but whatever time it takes for the reader to perceive his textual birth, the poet's body appearing in the reader's consciousness, the presence of both poet and reader needed together.

The presence of the body in the three poets' verses affects the reader so immediately as to take the breath away, the reader sometimes overwhelmed by Poe's ghoulish embodiments, Whitman's in-your-face beard and armpits, Dickinson's brash listings of lungs and blood and sinew and heart. Stoltzfus's discussion of Lacan includes a description of the act of reading that sees the reader forming his or her "own tropic network using the holes, traces, word repetitions" (8). The poetries of Poe, Whitman, and Dickinson enfold such holes and repetitions in the bodies of their texts: "Underlying all this is the voice of the Other caught in the folds of the text and which the reader unfolds so that the body can be heard and seen and touched and felt almost intuitively in what Barthes describes as orgasmic bliss (*jouissance*)" (Stoltzfus 8). It is through a kind of reader *jouissance* that the body of the poet, the body of the poem, is touched, the bliss providing a reaction that cannot be denied, and that sometimes occurs almost before the reader knows it. The three epigraphs that launch this chapter serve to capture moments of reader *jouissance* that find the body in the text—the rapture and attendant rupture that occurs in that moment. These moments ensure poetic longevity, and the legacy of Poe, Whitman, and Dickinson as writers of gendered language, feminine poetics, that will arrest readers for decades and centuries to come.

In "Tamerlane" Poe exemplifies his relationship to audience and language as the poem's main character tells his tale to a holy friar. The confessing friar, who must listen to the character and ultimately has the power to absolve him on the basis of his story, performs services parallel to those performed by the reader to the writer. On his deathbed Tamerlane tells his tale to the friar, a character bound by honor and profession to listen to the dying. Like the friar will keep, and forgive, Tamerlane's words even after he dies so will the reader transcend time barriers, but in this case, to decide whether to keep, and forgive, Poe's words.

"Why not a friar?" Poe asks in his footnote to "Tamerlane," betraying some vexation or artistic chafing concerning the placement of the frame story of confessor friar around the central adventure of "Tamerlane." He feels the need to justify the friar in his first footnote: "How shall I account for giving him [Tamerlane] 'a friar,' as a death-bed confessor—I cannot exactly determine. He wanted some one to listen to his tale—and why not a friar?" (26). He wants someone to listen to his tale: the dynamic directs us to what may be the primary, if unstated, story of "Tamerlane," a dynamic whereby the frame supersedes the center in importance.

Poe's willingness to consider after-death states prompts us to consider that he welcomed after-death audiences, and the dynamic of the frame story locates an almost ghoulish playfulness. Concerning Poe's stories, Renza claims that they "testify to the way he programs his texts to explode like time-bombs in the future" (81). I would further Renza's observation by enlarging the time-released nature of Poe's language to include his poems, and emphasize that my claim has more to do with the body of the reader and the feminine proclivities of Poe's poetry than with autobiographical traces of the author within his works, as Renza suggests.[2] Renza claims that "[t]he 'post-mortem effects,' as Lawrence implicitly termed them, of Poe's cryogenic project to survive by artificial textual means—through the galvanically, salty, or mesmerically induced misreadings coterminously defining the production of his texts—point to his willed plot to return to future readers as a ghostly autobiographical figure still haunting these texts" (82). In the poems, rather, we, as readers, find ourselves coopted into the poem, inhabiting the lines—in the case of "Tamerlane," in the person of the friar.

In one version of "Tamerlane" Poe goes so far as to assign us, the readers, dialogue, though we never speak the word, nor see it on the page. But the word is nonetheless said by the friar, because Tamerlane reacts in his otherwise unbroken soliloquy:

I have no time to dote or dream:
You call it hope—that fire of fire!
It is but agony of desire—
If I can hope (O God! I can)
Its fount is holier—more divine—
I would not call thee fool, old man,
But such is not a gift of thine. (45)

Here apparently the friar has told Tamerlane to hope, and Tamerlane reacts with anger; the word the friar—and we, by proxy—speak is "hope," though we never actually say it—but Tamerlane hears it. In the guise of the confessing friar we say our silent "hope," the "fire of fire" that can light creativity, and the speaker/Poe responds with the hope that he can find a holy desire. But then he plays rough with us readers, and comes close to calling us a foolish old man, chastising us with the reminder that what he can do is more divine than mere hoping—something he has a gift for, and we don't. Immediately after the above section he says, "Hear thou the secret of a spirit . . ." (45). At this point, the reader, promised a secret spirit, pays full attention.

Poe worked this device and tinkered with its effects a good deal. By attending to different versions we can see the amount of labor he invested in making us sit up and pay full attention. Tamerlane, dying, expresses surprise at having the friar/reader nearby to listen to him, but our presence is important because he reveals to us his secret:

The gay wall of this gaudy tower
Grows dim around me—death is near.
I had not thought, until this hour
When passing from the earth, that ear
Of any, were it not the shade
Of one whom in life I made
All mystery but a simple name,
Might know the secret of a spirit
Bow'd down in sorrow, and in shame.—
Shame said'st thou? (27)

Here stands in full the fragment of epigraph launching this chapter. In the deathbed scene Poe has something to whisper to us—his last words—and we are the ear Tamerlane had "not thought" he would have. Again we are assigned dialogue: "Shame?" we say, though again, silently. Whether we like it or not we are inscribed in this dim scenario, so that our reading of it necessitates our recognition of ourselves as readers of Poe. Later in the poem, Poe may address the imbedded reader within parentheses:

(I speak thus openly to thee,
'Twere folly *now* to veil a thought
With which this aching breast is fraught) . . . (32)

He has warmed up in the course of the poem, and now speaks openly to us. The middle word of the parenthetical lines, "*now*," realizes simultaneously the now of Tamerlane's moment of speaking, probably the now of Poe's writing of it, and the changeable "now" of the reader as we take on the friar's role, regardless of generation or century.

Whitman, too, establishes a tie of timelessness between himself and the reader of his poetry, as he does, famously, in "Crossing Brooklyn Ferry": "What is it then between us?" Typically the question he has to ask us, the inquiry broaches betweenness on spatial, psychological, sexual, and temporal terms. With absolute immediacy he queries the reader, point blank, and clarifies that the answer may take decades or centuries to answer. His body, however, is what matters in answering the question,[3] for he has been struck from the float, and has received his identity by way of his body: "That I was I knew was of my body, and what I should be I knew I should be of my body" (Bradley and Blodgett 162). Hence, the fifth section of "Crossing Brooklyn Ferry" begins by asking the reader about the body as text—"What is it then between us?"—and ends by answering what the reader should or, when ready, in the right century, *will* probably answer: "Whatever it is, it avails not—" because we know what we are of our body.

The strategy remains particularly vexed. The three poets grapple with signification that remains in the mode of the Father, by recourse to the body that remains in the mode of the mother. They manifest authenticity in their texts by the measure of the wordless in the body, the patriarchal signifier finding reality because of the *choric* pulsions and possibilities of being struck from the float.[4] Dickinson, in turn, grapples with the interplay of patriarchal signification and maternal gesture, in the poem, "I've dropped my Brain—My Soul is numb—" (Fr1088), partially cited as an epigraph for this chapter. In the poem the speaker's body dies, or effects a kind of life-in-death stance whereby the soul is numb, the veins are palsied, and paralysis overtakes the speaker as if she were a statue, "Done perfecter on stone." As a statue her vitality is "Carved and cool" and her nerve is marble; even though she is a statue she is capable, paradoxically, of being "moved," and has "Instincts for Dance—a caper part—/ An Aptitude for Bird—." She has a proclivity for singing—that is to say making poetry—but someone, never identified, has stilled her voice and her body:

Who wrought Carrara in me
And chiselled all my tune
Were it a Witchcraft—were it Death—
I've still a chance to strain

To Being, somewhere—Motion—Breath—
Though Centuries beyond,
And every limit a Decade—
I'll shiver, satisfied. (Fr1088)

Dickinson asks her readers a question: Who turned me into stone, making my song incapable of being heard? As with Poe and Whitman, it is because readers might perceive her body that her question eventually might be answered and her song heard. As with Whitman it may take decades or centuries before Dickinson finds the right audience, but till then she remains contented to let her song stay within her body; the embodiedness of the poem—straining, motion, breath—imports the exactitude of the task of presenting the text. The shivering in the final line is crucial to Dickinson's major criterion for poetry—that is, it makes the reader so cold s/he can never get warm again. Here, the writer must do the shivering until the reader is ready.

It may take a long time; meanwhile, the signifiers obscure and veil the body, language existing as a kind of scrim over the realm of the feminine, still hidden. The body is veiled in the occlusion of the feminine that enables patriarchal language systems, but Poe and Whitman and Dickinson begin, in a dramatic way, to find renewed readers—those readers who can discern the feminine. As they wink at us we begin to take on the shiver, to strike ourselves from the float, and to act as their confessing friar, in order to perceive in their works not only the word, but beyond that, a kind of maternal language. Through them we can reclaim the feminine body and the mother, and lean toward the matronymic expression that is trembling, unpronounceable, and crucially unnameable.

Poe seeks "that ear of any" reader willing to discern the secret that defines his longevity; Whitman seeks the reader who will acknowledge and prize what is between the writer and reader; Dickinson seeks the reader who will forge "Centuries beyond" to apprehend the feminine. The quality of the beyond locates these poets for their audience—whichever generation happens currently to be reading them. Why not designate a reader-friar who can act as confessor to a poet? Why not suggest an anonymous audience—"whoever you are"—in order to ascertain the pulsions of the sea that initiate birth for a poet who is a mother-man? Why not create a female statue that revives as we witness her shivering between the dashes? In these ways, Poe, Whitman, and Dickinson move beneath and between the signifier of patriarchal language, as they limn for us a poetry of otherness that depends upon our apperception of what exists underneath the word.

Notes

꧁ꕥ꧂

INTRODUCTION

1. The first two epigraphs are from Johnson's edition of Emily Dickinson letters by page numbers (L649, L404). The third is quoted from Eric Carlson's *In Recognition of Edgar Allan Poe* (73).

Subsequently, all phrases and lines from Whitman poems will be quoted from Cowley, followed by page number, unless the poem was written after 1855, in which case it will be quoted from Bradley and Blodgett, indicated by the last names Bradley and Blodgett, with page number. All quotations from Poe's poems, unless otherwise indicate. are taken from Mabbott and are followed by the page number from that edition when first cited. All Dickinson quotations are taken from Franklin's three-volume variorum, followed by poem number, or from Franklin's manuscripts, indicated by title.

2. This pronouncement of Whitman by Dickinson follows immediately on the heels of her anxiety that her art doesn't please him: "But I fear my story fatigues you" (L404). The tone of ribbing is reminiscent of Dickinson's tone when she has fun at the expense of her father, as when she reports that her father buys her books but begs her not to read them.

3. Furthermore, Sherry Ceniza, concerning the possibility of Dickinson having been familiar with Whitman, states that Dickinson "could hardly have missed" (121) a particular review of *Leaves of Grass* in *The Springfield Republican* that referred to Whitman's book as "smut." Vivian Pollak, in "Whitman's Visionary Feminism," goes even further: "We don't know if Dickinson ever read Whitman's 'Book,' though she is likely to have read "As I Ebb'd with the Ocean of Life' when it ap-

peared in April 1860 in the *Atlantic Monthly*, to which she and her family sub-scribed" (104).

4. For instance, "I tend my flowers for thee" (Fr367) and "In Winter in my Room" (Fr1742) seem nearly pornographic by nineteenth-century standards, and read with equal force in comparison to Whitman's erotic sequences.

5. Silverman notes that Poe may have met Whitman (486n).

6. Johnson notes of a Dickinson thank-you letter to Henry V. Emmons, an in-terpretation of Dickinson's use of the words "pearl, onyx, and emerald." The first let-ter of each word spells "Poe,"perhaps as a kind of acrostic to thank Emmons for a volume of Poe poetry (L303).

7. Tufariello, though, makes important distinctions, such as the following: "But she [Dickinson] implicitly rejected the organic metaphors for poetry that pervade *Nature* and that so appealed to Whitman" (177).

8. Needless to say, the ongoing discussions about sexuality concerning each of these authors is vexed. Poe, for instance, broke few cultural expectations when he married his first cousin, a choice not unusual in the 1800s, though he would have raised eyebrows by marrying a bride so extremely young. Whether Whitman should be referred to as homosexual, homoerotic, or, as he was some decades ago, omnierotic, is continually undergoing discussion, even within the body of work by each critic. See, for example, Robert K. Martin on rethinking his views on Whit-man's homosexuality in "Whitman and the Politics of Identity." Some of the major critics discussing Dickinson's homoeroticism or homosexuality are Rebecca Patterson, Lilian Faderman, Paula Bennett, and Martha Nell Smith.

9. As an aside, Williams provides an interesting observation concerning the no-tion of the "I" or the self, in Poe's stories: "The 'selves' that inhabit Poe's tales are fundamentally equivocal. His tales place in question the primary assumption of a unified self that language behind Common-Sense philosophy, which as Terence Martin has shown, permeated American intellectual discussion in the early nine-teenth century" (17).

10. This last category, though—mysteries and riddles—applies more to Dickinson than to Whitman.

11. For example, Joan Dayan and Paula Kot have studied the image of the female body in Poe. M. Jimmie Killingsworth, Michael Moon, and Vivian Pollak, to name a very few of many, have explored the body in Whitman's work. Even F.O. Matthiessen, as early as 1941, was aware of Whitman as a poet of the body: "No one before the protomodern Whitman understood the body's 'immediate bearing upon living speech' " (523). Dickinson has been amply studied as a poet of the body by Gilbert and Gubar, Mary Loeffelholz, Martha Nell Smith, and many others.

12. The claim of Whitman and Dickinson as experimental has been advanced by James Olney, who sees Dickinson's "slant" poetry in conjunction with Whitman's "indirect" poetry of America (44).

13. The two versions of Fr277 also form an absorbing study of experimentations in gender and point of view. Whereas the first version begins with the line, "Going to

Him! Happy letter!" the second version begins with the line, "Going—to—Her!" The line placements and punctuations, and some word variants, distinguish the two poems in interesting and cross-gendering ways.

14. I borrow the phrase "choosing not choosing" from the title of Sharon Cameron's defining and indispensable book on Dickinson's fascicles. As Cameron explains, one of the benefits of "choosing not choosing" is that it can confer different kinds of power: that of "demarcating identity" and that of excluding nothing (153). One is a "discrete identity, the other predicated on identity that is inclusive, even illusorily infinite" (154).

15. Kahn also draws an extremely useful distinction between "the language of birth" and its opposite, pointing out that the former applies to "*the birth of cities, the birth of nations*" (5). She calls for a consideration of the opposite: "But what about a language of birth? For the phrase *the language of* holds generative power as well" (5). Kahn believes conventional medical vocabulary disfigures the maternal body, and that a new language is called for.

CHAPTER 1: POE'S "THE RAVEN" AND GESTATIVE SIGNIFICATION

1. I find Salska's study somewhat Whitman-loaded, besides leaning on Emerson where Emerson is sometimes not helpful. (Emerson, for all his advantages, simply is not the cogent choice as the father of American literature once minorities and women are included; in other words, "Self-Reliance" was not written for minorities—or if it were, it would be a rather cruel tract.)

2. The most compelling reason for preferring Poe to Emerson in a study of nineteenth-century poets concerns Emerson's views on language, by which the word is vehicular, implying a carrier and a carried, signifier and signified—a fitting—and none of the three poets studied here would claim such succinct relations in language. Salska does examine Emerson's "Poetry and Imagination," a later essay, to find that he "believes, at least in this essay, that in the beginning there was impulse or beat rather than word" (165)—an intriguing observation concerning language. As Salska points out, though, because the essay was published in 1876, "it must be that Whitman arrived more or less independently at the idea or intuition that language is first of all rhythmic motion" (165).

3. These risks, I think, are different from Emerson's transcendence, which proposes movement to a more unified reality, available, purportedly, to everyone. Dickinson and Poe do not share Emerson's optimism in *Nature*, for example, that there is nothing that will not some day be understood. Dickinson and Whitman show themselves to be far more sexual and bawdy than Emerson, and Whitman understood that Emerson grievously misread him when he advised Whitman to omit from *Leaves of Grass* all the parts having to do with the body. Moreover, all three show fascinating cross-genderings lacking in Emerson. Whitman and Dickinson play with taking on the personae of both genders, and Poe addresses vexed gender questions. Emerson believes in the poet as spermatic man, disseminating words in the

world; while Whitman clearly shares this spermatic generosity and bluster, he also longs for female generativity as well.

4. Even biographical anecdotes show Poe, Whitman, and Dickinson considering themselves oppositionally to Emerson. Whitman enraged Emerson when he turned the latter's private congratulations public, by including them without asking permission on the spine of his new edition of *Leaves of Grass*; friends of Emerson claimed the occasion of Whitman's presumption was the only time they had seen Emerson so angry he couldn't speak. Dickinson, in turn, knew Emerson was visiting her brother and sister-in-law next door at the Evergreens, but chose not to walk the few steps there to meet him. Whitman's and Dickinson's works reflect these independent attitudes and actions taken toward the writer usually thought to be the father of American letters.

5. Dayan, in a different work, also states, tellingly, that it is unsettling that issues of gender (and race) "have not figured much in criticism of Poe's writings" (*Face* 196).

6. Davidson proceeds to say this about Poe, Whitman, and Dickinson: "Different as at first consideration those three poets were, they were nonetheless very similar—certainly Poe and Whitman were—in their search for a unitary theory of the universe of man and God. Poe was different from them too; he was never touched by the profound reaches of the Puritan mind in quest of its own private center, as was Emily Dickinson; and, despite the influences of German transcendental thought and idealistic philosophy, Poe, unlike Whitman, always remained half-rationalist and half-organicist" (44).

7. Carton goes on to add the following: "Thus, Poe's narrators are balloonists, addicts, hypnotics, historians of the future, victims of mental or physical disease, murderers of victims intimately associated with themselves, doomed or dead men, and disembodied spirits" (15).

8. An illustration from one of the most innocuous seeming of Poe's productions of verse, "To————" (Version B of "To Marie Louise") highlights Poe's unequivocal fascination with the cusp between language and what is beyond language. I quote from the second version:

Not long ago, the writer of these lines,
In the mad pride of intellectuality,
Maintained the "power of words"—denied that ever
A thought arose within the human brain
Beyond the utterance of the human tongue;
And now, as if in mockery of that boast,
Two words—two foreign soft dissyllables—

Have stirred from out the abysses of his heart,
Unthought-like thoughts that are the souls of thought,
Richer, far wilder, far diviner visions
Than even the seraph harper, Israfel,
Who has "the sweetest voice of all God's creatures,"

Could hope to utter. And I! My spells are broken.
The pen falls powerless from my shivering hand. (406–7)

It is a love poem—a light love poem, by Poe's standards—and yet the fact that even here Poe concerns himself essentially with questions of what lies beyond signification shows his power as a poet of marginalized naming. In this poem Poe identifies the failures and necessary alternatives and differences of signifying that poets in the next century or two will experience. The name or signifer is the one he cannot speak, "beyond the utterance of the human tongue," that apparently no one can speak:

With thy dear name as text, though bidden by thee,
I cannot write—I cannot speak or think,
Alas, I cannot feel; for 'tis not feeling,
This standing motionless upon the golden
Threshold of the wide-open gate of dreams . . . (407–8; B)

Renza mentions, in reference to the tales, Poe's use of what seems like "anonymous signifiers" (76), and the same might be said here for the poems, even in such a relatively slight poem as this. "With thy dear name as text," the poem claims, writing and speaking are no longer possible, and what fascinates and confounds the reader is that we don't know what the name is. This is a poem, as with many of Poe's seemingly unexceptional poems, not to be neglected, because it can offer rewarding insights regarding the name that is text that cannot be written or spoken. The poem catches up several worthy Poe-esque themes: powerless pens, dreamscapes, the strength of the feminine, the anticipation of *chora*-like pulsions, the failures of language, and the "anonymous signifiers."

9. Renza's article argues that Matthiessen buries Poe's "body" of work in a footnote of *American Renaissance*, prematurely burying him "in the archives of American literary history" (85). Concerning claiming Poe from the French, Renza's ghostly tone and wit are just right: "And it is this 'influence,' albeit subterranean, which suggests that Poe's 'body' of works, continually purloined by French criticism, was in fact produced in such a way as to return to its original American ideological setting—if only to haunt it and engender readings possessing the uncanny effect of a séance" (85).

10. All Poe references are from Thomas Ollive Mabbott, in *Collected Works of Edgar Allan Poe*, Vol. I, *Poems*, in this case from page 369. Hereafter references to Poe's poetry, unless otherwise indicated, will be cited from Mabbott, with the page number given parenthetically.

11. I am grateful to those who have explored language and desire in Edgar Allan Poe's "The Raven," as for example, Kennedy, Blasing, Williams, Humphries, and especially Elmer. Kennedy sees importance in the name "Lenore," which "signifies the absence which afflicts him [the narrator]" (68). Blasing understands "Lenore" as representing a maternal, "natural" source language (28); basically, Blasing offers a brief discussion of the poem as a Kristevan struggle between the maternal and paternal forces of language, between the names "Lenore" and "Nevermore." Williams argues

that the "Nevermore" is essentially empty and though it "seems to be a potential in-cursion of meaning from a supernal realm [it] is significant only in the context of the lover's narrative of loss" (7). Humphries concludes his discussion of "Poe-eticity" by remarking that, "*raven* is a name for the point at which signification breaks down and literariness, if it is to occur, will occur. It is the locus of the purely other, death, or whatever cipher one chooses to paste over its absence. It must be articulated in terms combining a tension of resemblance and difference, short of nothingness but sufficiently different so that the dialectic, or circuit, of signification is engaged, while it remains extraordinary, incongruous—in the extreme, grotesque" (59). Finally, Jonathan Elmer, in greater detail than the above critics, explores the use of the signifier in "The Raven," as both "the very type of the arbitrary signifier," and the re-cording of "the narrator's gradual assimilation to meaning of the bird's initially senseless repetition of the word" (204–5). While I entertain some disagreements with the above critics, overall I appreciate their work that opens up ways of thinking about "The Raven" as a text that explores a sophisticated scenario of language.

12. The citation is from the translation of Lacan's major work, *Écrits: A Selection*, page 303. All subsequent references to Lacan will be to *Écrits* unless otherwise desig-nated within the text.

13. There are other indications, too. Though the narrator is surrounded by books, they all contain "forgotten lore," the erasure of words. As he turns each inked page, imaged as the "uncertain rustling of each purple curtain" (365)—more veil than elucidation, uncertain as opposed to clear—the absence becomes apparent.

14. This appears, however, only in the French edition of *Écrits*.

15. For Freud's description of the *Fort! Da!* game, see Freud's "Beyond the Plea-sure Principle," in his complete works, Vol. 18, page 3.

16. Humphries sees a temporal disjunction: "*Never* is a negative name of eter-nity, pointing to past and future. *More* is similarly limitless, but acts as a positive and temporally specific limitation, a contradiction, of this negative infinity (never). The tension between the words establishes a difference between the past (a hypothetically pure anteriority) and the present, and it is this dialectical difference that the poem's analepses enact" (62).

17. Taylor Stoehr comments on Poe's sense of reality as based on a kind of word reality, noting that Poe "attempts a language that is absolutely literal. In Poe's solipsistic world all reality will ultimately rest on words" (322).

18. Joseph Riddel observes that "the power of words is no more than a power to move other words. Words are already secondary, and they repeat only an original abysm that marks their distance from any first law" (122). Riddel goes on to remark that this "is a fable that Poe obsessively retells, the wearying struggle to purify lan-guage through language, the poetic repetition of some idea of 'absolute perfection' or some idea of purity that in the same gesture reveals the mark of its own discontinuity with any original form, idea, truth, reality" (122).

19. Often I'll use the phrase Oedipal "scenario," rather than Oedipal "dilemma" or "complex," so as to distance and even ironize somewhat the usage of the phrase.

First of all, I suspect that language acquisition does not work exactly this way for women though it may well for men and for the male narrator of "The Raven." Second and more importantly, I want to emphasize the language propensities, as opposed to the biological, that operate here. Lacan claims to work only in the realm of language, but sometimes biologism seems to creep in. For instance, Lacan believes that both male and female infants experience the want-to-be—especially as he distinguishes between the "phallus" and the "penis" (as symbol versus sexual organ)—and yet integral to his formulations is the assertion that the mother does not have the phallus or the penis. This is just one example of his claimed distinction between metaphor and biologism turning into essentialism. As a metaphor for language, the oedipal movements work well to reveal desire; where Lacan clearly works with the metaphorical is the ground on which I wish to stand.

20. I should mention that the narrator refers to the raven as "it" again in line 62, presumably because the gender change is difficult to apprehend all at once (367). In the final three lines of the poem, however, Poe designates the raven twice by using masculine pronouns, and makes the bird's male gender strikingly clear (369).

21. Humphries offers a useful discussion of the character of the word "raven": it contains "rave" and hints of "ravage"; backward, the word is "nevar." Poe chose "raven" for its "exotic ugliness and its association in many folk traditions with ill fortune." In addition, Mallarmé translated the word to the French *corbeau*, which sustains a pun on *corps beau* (beautiful body, or beautiful corpse). The French *corbeau* means both raven and crow, the latter a smaller, more common, less ominous bird (Humphries 51). Hence, to French eyes *corbeau* has many overtones and slippages the English word could never have.

22. Nineteenth-century audiences focused on Pallas Athena as a spooky element in the poem. Notice, for example, the following account by an "English Miss Barrett": "I hear of persons *haunted* by the Nevermore, and one acquaintance of mine, who has the misfortune of possessing a bust of Pallas, never can bear to look at it in the twilight" (cited in Carlson 23).

23. Sandra Gilbert and Susan Gubar, noting Ann Douglas's study of the nineteenth-century cult of death, discuss the "killing of women into art" in *Madwoman in the Attic*. For a recent survey of scholarship concerning Poe's women, see Paula Kot's "Feminist 'Re-Visioning' of the Tales of Women." Kot describes the split between critics who see Poe as misogynist, damned especially by his claim that the most poetical topic is a dying woman, and those who see him as commenting on his culture's representation of women. Kot notes that "more recently, critics argue that Poe did, indeed, know better, that he did not simply reinscribe conventional (repressive) attitudes toward women but that he critiqued these attitudes in his tales"(388).

24. Actually, Lenore appears again in the fourteenth and sixteenth (the prepenultimate) stanzas. In the fourteenth, the narrator has forged his memories of Lenore into a distant second person (he refers to himself in the second person): "thy memories of Lenore" (368). In the prepenultimate, we seem to have the Lenore of

the beginning, the Lenore whom the angels have named. It is perhaps significant, though, that Poe actually wrote this stanza first (*Essays* 20).

25. The accentuated reliance upon the three elements of bird, bust, and chamber door may anticipate the triadic elements (of bird, star, and lilac) in Whitman's "When Lilacs Last in the Dooryard Bloom'd"; Whitman may use the elements for oedipal resonances, too.

26. And perhaps it is important that the raven perches atop the bust—that he, as phallus on phallus, has what she is only perceived to be; or perhaps Lacan would have it so.

27. Poe reported to his friend Mrs. Weiss that he considered the word "lining" a "blunder," but "was unwilling to sacrifice the whole stanza" (373). The "blunder" strikes me as one of those fortunate mistakes that reveals Poe's oedipal scenario; in any case, it is interesting that he felt he couldn't revise the one word without jettisoning the entire stanza.

28. I offer thanks to my colleague, Mark Richardson, for clarifying added possibilities in this section.

29. The double quotation mark at the start of the line is added for clarity's sake, given that the quotation began in a previous line. The first printing of the poem, in the *American Review: A Whig Journal of Politics, Literature, Art and Science I* (February 1845), cites line 66 as follows: "That sad answer, 'Nevermore!' " (369–70). This rendering involves the narrator in the saying of the signifier even less than the stuttered line, as again he only reports what the raven says. It should be noted that many variations of the poem exist, and that Poe continued to revise this much-reprinted poem for the rest of his life. The version of "The Raven" here follows Mabbott's use of the Richmond *Semi-Weekly Examiner*, "the last authorized version published during Poe's lifetime" (364).

30. Although the stutter occurs near the end of the second section, the occurrence does blur somewhat the tripartite division that does not have the narrator (almost) speaking until the third section. This discrepancy may account additionally for the stutter.

31. To the writer's activity—that of taking up the black plume—the raven/father replies with an enigmatic "Nevermore." This may or may not suggest the person of John Allan, Poe's adoptive father, who seemed to say "no," a kind of "Nevermore," to many of Poe's most heartfelt activities.

32. Poe's uses of stillness are legion, not only in "The Raven" but in many of his poems, as discussed in Chapter Four.

CHAPTER 2: WHITMAN'S "SONG OF MYSELF" AND GESTATIVE SIGNIFICATION

1. Herein follows an extended list of Whitman's pregnancy terms: enclose, dilation, development, growing, increase, unfolding, plenty, nest, eggs (of many kinds), incorporate, expand, assume, embody, plenum, afflatus, omnific, debouch, "procreant urge," "spheric product," "en masse," and more.

2. I am indebted to several critics who read Whitman's poetry as poetry of the body, among them M. Jimmie Killingsworth, Tenney Nathanson, and Michael Moon. Killingsworth enters into discussions of maternity in Whitman's poetry, though not specifically in "Song of Myself," with Whitman as active mother. Nathanson understands Whitman's body of poetry as fluid and "assuming" different shapes, but not as concerns motherhood. I am especially grateful for Moon's notion of specularity and recognition of Whitman's modulations between fluid and solid; Moon also sees Whitman's eroticism as more indeterminate and hence more interesting than heretofore perceived.

3. All citations in this chapter refer to line assignations taken from Malcolm Cowley's edition of Walt Whitman's "Song of Myself" in the 1855 *Leaves of Grass*, unless indicated, with page number following.

4. The importance of hydropathy to Whitman has been noted by Reynolds (Beneath 333) and others, but Sherry Ceniza notes the impact of *The Water-Cure Journal* on Whitman: "Evidence of the journal's influence on Whitman surfaces on a linguistic level in his use of the word 'accouchement,' a term regularly used in the journal" (131).

5. In fact, the fifth section encrypts elements of natural childbirth in its ambiguous and sexually saturated rendering of human experience. It may not be going too far to wonder if Whitman depicts labor as well as the other possibilities of sexual behavior, such as deep kissing or "embracing? fellatio? penetration?" (Moon 48).

6. Kenneth Price suggests that section twenty-five acts as a kind of replay of section five (50–51).

7. Whitman had a penchant for using fold imagery as a way to suggest the female body, as most notably in "Unfolded Out of the Folds," with its first line, "Unfolded out of the folds of the woman man comes unfolded and is always to come unfolded" (Bradley and Blodgett 391).

8. Ceniza proceeds to state that the Whitman persona "lies next to the woman, close, in a way like present-day practice in which the male shares in the birthing experience as much as he can" (110).

9. It is also important to point out that Cixous warns against male cooptation of the maternal function of childbirth: "Let us demater-paternalize rather than deny woman, in an effort to avoid the co-optation of procreation, a thrilling era of the body. Let us defetishize" ("Medusa" 294).

CHAPTER 3: DICKINSON'S FASCICLE TWENTY-EIGHT AND GESTATIVE SIGNIFICATION

1. There are notable exceptions, of course; for only one example, Sylvia Plath includes the unborn, in "Ouija" and "Three Women."

2. William Shurr constructs a biography for Dickinson by using selected poems, and while he offers the caveat that he is more interested in the poems than in biography, his critical rhetoric reads like a narrative, as if we the readers have been drawn into a secret story about the author. Barbara Murray's dissertation, "The *Scar-*

let Experiment," directed by Shurr, argues that Dickinson herself had an abortion. I strongly differentiate my study from these studies, and would claim to operate, critically, much closer to Jerome Loving's observation that consideration of the issue enhances an appreciation of the poetry: "A recent critical fantasy suggests that Dickinson became pregnant (perhaps by Wadsworth) and even underwent an abortion. Although the theory is far-fetched, its value as a key to Dickinson's ontology is nevertheless useful" (92).

3. Such a claim would be tantamount to asserting that because Dickinson wrote of death that she died before the writing of each such poem, or that because she wrote of the sea, that it is imperative she traveled there.

4. Unfortunately, there is little information on miscarriage, as opposed to abortion. Degler cites one doctor, reporting in 1889, "'that more than one-half of the human family dies before it is born, and that probably three-fourths of these premature deaths are the direct or indirect result of abortion by intent' " (231). The same seems to be true today—that miscarriages are much more difficult to record than abortions. Women may miscarry early in the term, before becoming aware of pregnancy. Hence, much of the ensuing discussion will focus on abortion as opposed to what the medical community calls spontaneous abortion, or miscarriage, as the latter is more difficult to record.

5. I use Franklin's manuscript books for all of the poems cited from Fascicles Twenty-Seven, Twenty-Eight, and Twenty-Nine, though I rely, for convenience's sake, upon Franklin's variorum edition for poems outside of these three fascicles. Hence, I refer to fascicle poems by the first line of the poem as the poem appears in the manuscript books. Upon first mention of the poem I supply the variorum numbering of the poem for easy cross-referencing.

6. Although historians assert that the emotional climate concerning abortion was not nearly as charged in the middle nineteenth century as it was later in the century with the passage of the Comstock Laws, still the issue couldn't help but raise questions. Dickinson's questions in this poem anticipate the complexity of Gwendolyn Brooks's poem on abortion, "The Mother," which avoids polemics, assuming a stance of neither "pro-life" nor "pro-choice," as we would phrase it today. Dickinson, nearly 100 years earlier, also refused to resort to easy solutions, evincing both delicacy and unflinching resolve in representing difficult decisions and emotions.

7. Sharon Cameron asserts that a poem in different contexts is not the same poem (6).

8. Martha Nell Smith, in *Rowing in Eden*, also provides an eloquent voice for reading Dickinson in manuscript versions (though she does not address the fascicles primarily). Similarly to Cameron, Smith examines the "same" poem in two different contexts and comes to different conclusions, thus "leaving a single definite text indeterminate [which] makes the poem more, not less, exciting to the general reader, and more, not less, interesting to the literary scholar" (69).

9. It seems to me possible, for example, that "I pay—in Satin Cash—" (526), the second poem in Fascicle Twenty-Eight, was added because there was room for a small poem in that space. The handwriting and pen marking are noticeably different. This doesn't mean, however, that Dickinson squeezed any poem randomly into that space. Presumably she had many four-line poems from which to choose. Similarly, the blank page-and-a-half after the eighth poem in the fascicle may have been saved for a poem, too, but Dickinson may not have had one of that length to fit thematically or imagistically with the others in the fascicle. The ordering of poems in a fascicle may be nothing more than the shuffling of a creative mind—but that is hardly a random shuffling. It may be, in fact, nothing *less* than the shuffling of a creative mind.

10. Werner adds the following: "Here deciphering gives way to witnessing: its labor is to make explicit something unprecedented—and, in the process, to reveal the acts of writing and silent reading as visual poems" (16).

11. I don't believe that the poems' grouping is always so consciously deliberate as it is associatively arranged, whether formally or informally. Sometimes the arrangement includes considerations such as the size of the poem, clusters of images, and to some extent loose chronology. I do not see the fascicles as always so constructedly unconstructed as Cameron seems to argue at times they are, but I do see them as being so multivalenced.

12. The organic metaphor is used as the premise for M. Jimmie Killingsworth's entire book on Walt Whitman, *The Growth of Leaves of Grass: The Organic Tradition in Whitman Studies*.

13. Margaret Homans and Cristanne Miller, among others, have discussed the circumstance of Dickinson writing the body. For instance, Robert McClure Smith suggests that "the poetry of Emily Dickinson clearly derives from the antebellum period's own version of *ecriture feminine* [*sic*]" (128). Paula Bennett has examined *jouissance* in Dickinson's poetry and Mary Loeffelholz has contextualized Dickinson within the spectrum of feminist thought.

14. From this point on I will use primarily the word "abortion" to refer to the possibility of abortion or miscarriage, as the word "abortion" is used medically to refer to either. (As noted above, doctors refer to miscarriage as "spontaneous abortion.")

15. Paul Crumbley's *Inflections of the Pen* examines heteroglossia throughout.

16. Temma Berg, though, offers a variation on this theme: "The feminine becomes the realm of the artist of either sex: a realm of the Word itself. The feminine is what fills and empties meaning. On the other hand, there are indications that Kristeva, like Irigaray, sees the feminine as a special difference that functions in a woman's practice" (14).

17. The characteristic line Dickinson drew after a poem entry is missing for this the manuscript poem.

18. The word "Estimate" locates an important thematic concern in the fascicle, because of its evocation of the counting of uncountable things. An integral part of

Fascicle Twenty-Eight, counting appears time and again in the forms of telling, reckoning, wondering how many, brokering, measuring, gain, tendering, taking the balance (including also words of measurement such as price, legions, units, cubits, and bullion). In "He gave away his Life—" the counting of the first stanza offers a way to attempt to account for the "Gigantic Sum" that is a life.

19. Lambert uses the 1844 Webster, *An American Dictionary of the English Language* (30), for his manual of Dickinson's legal terms. Whicher uses the 1847 Webster, which he states is "the lexicon she studied" (232), but Wolff argues that Whicher did not have access to the Lyman letters, which help to date Dickinson's lexicon as the 1828 Webster. Accordingly, I take my definitions from the 1828 *American Dictionary*.

20. Upon closer inspection we find that the word has been inked over another faint word that appears to have been erased, which Franklin identifies as "way." The palimpsest shows a convergence of the organic "process," perhaps with the Christian "way," just one instance of the converged and dual Dickinson we discover in the fascicles.

21. A poem outside the fascicle, "It would never be Common—more—I said—" (Fr388), augments an interpretation of "common" as ironized. This poem has been read variously as a fairy tale, as a poem describing a writer finding her inspiration, and as a poem of gothic rape, the latter of which I argue in *Emily Dickinson's Gothic* (86–88). It probably contains all those possibilities but, interestingly for our purposes, the speaker describes her "uncommon" experience in terms of parturition. She acknowledges that "it sometime—showed—as 'twill—," and feels "so much joy—I told it—Red—" even though "'Twas needless—any speak—." She claims, "I walked—as wings—my body bore—." At the end of the poem, however, the sackcloth and frock hang loose, showing her "tenantless" body. The speaker misses her "drop" of brightness, not unlike the tint of red or scarlet freight of the poems discussed above, and the common/uncommon experience of pregnancy has ended, here, in loss.

22. Spontaneous bursting from a pod: curiously, it's a condition Lacan rehearses in his consideration of "dehiscence," and what Michael Payne calls "the most striking of Lacan's biological metaphors," used to designate "the spontaneous opening of the structure of a ripe plant" (Payne 31). Dickinson's breaking from a pod may anticipate Lacan's dehiscence, which refers to "the intersection of the mental and natural worlds" (Payne 31). As such it provides an engaging terminology to apply to Emily Dickinson's biological terms. Her use of the word "pod" also indicates an intersection of mental and natural worlds in that it refers to signification and interrupted-term parturition at the same time.

23. It is worth noting that in the fascicle the word "now—," in the penultimate line, appears to be added on. Perhaps Dickinson originally liked the reverse slant-rhyme of "Deluge" and "legend" that would have concluded the last two lines of the poem; both words carry three of the same consonants in a different order. As the word "now" interrupts the linkage of "Deluge" and "legend," there must have been an overriding reason for Dickinson to have added it. The temporal cue "now"

may accentuate the difference between the personal investment (of Noah) and the cultural investment in myth that may erase the individual.

24. The white space forms an admirable prelude for "I reckon—when I count" (Fr533), perhaps the most famous poem in the fascicle. The blankness invites the reader to fill it, to consider this and "The Winters are so short—" together, thematically, as bookends to the blank page and a half. In the earlier poem the winters were short; here the summer lasts a year. In the earlier, Noah wasn't credited; here the poet is everything and gets not only full credit but all the credit. The counting in this poem feeds successfully into the question about counting in the following poem, "How many Flowers fail in Wood—," and the subsequent poem, "It might be lonelier" (Fr535), in which the speaker imagines "Land in Sight—," although she herself is still out to sea. All three consecutive poems, then, tracked from Noah through land in sight, serve as preparation for the final "pod" poem, "My first well Day—since," in which the speaker returns to life after a season of reclusion.

25. "Summer—we all have seen—" is closely tied with another poem in Fascicle Twenty-Eight, "They dropped like Flakes—" (Fr545), recalling "How many Flowers fail in Wood—." In both, natural objects, occurring multitudinously, are expended.

26. Summer is described in sliding similes compared to our adversity, perversity, obliquity, extremity: this poem exhibits an in-progress and fragmented state at the extreme. The possible choices for many of the words, phrases, and lines make the argument that the poem has any one definitive reading preposterous.

27. I honor Dickinson's gaps here, allying myself with Cristanne Miller's study of Dickinson's grammar, in which she proposes the phrase, "nonrecoverable deletion," to indicate the sites in Dickinson's poems where indeterminacy renders meaning not recuperable.

28. Benfey discusses this poem in which "tickets are requisite for admission to the grave" (42), adding that "[t]he 'two' that the tickets admit are, I assume, body and soul, Bearer and Borne, and only the body remains seated" (43).

29. She doesn't tell us the syllable, though; perhaps it is not even a word; perhaps it is preverbal babble, perhaps postverbal babble. The syllable the dying speak may be the word "tea," which could follow as a syntactical consequence in the poem. "Tea," further, could commensurate the letter "T," a possibility for signifying several important words in the poem: True, Tomb, tell, or two (the relation of bearer to borne). All of these words form apt candidates for describing the nature of language. It's not difficult to imagine the dying uttering as a farewell message any one of these "T" syllables.

30. As an aside, the final poems of Fascicles Twenty-Seven and Twenty-Nine end also with devastating uncertainty. The last poem of Fascicle Twenty-Seven is of cosmic scope, huge and nihilistic; the last of Fascicle Twenty-Nine is, if possible, even more nihilistic and terminating. Knowing this makes the unsteadiness of the ending poem of Fascicle Twenty-Eight resound all the more.

31. Two of Dickinson's poems from outside Fascicle Twenty-Eight mention Nicodemus. Nicodemus asked Jesus how one "'can enter the second time into his mother's womb, and be born?'" (John 3.4, cited in Johnson 100). Poem Fr90 in-

vokes "a flower expected everywhere—" in a landscape of mystery and expectancy, before "Nicodemus' Mystery" solves the riddle in the penultimate line. Poem Fr1218 invokes "Nicodemus' Phantom" in trying to find the marrow of the bone as a metaphor for the center of "A Being," possibly a figuration for parturition. In these poems Dickinson works to coopt rebirth, a staple of Christianity, and to depict unusual circumstances of pregnancy, such as arrested term pregnancy.

CHAPTER 4: WORD, BIRTH, AND POE'S ALCHEMY

1. This shifting among women's proper names hints at the matrilineal, an example of which occurs in the short story "Ligeia." In that tale, it is true that the inheritance is not passed woman to woman, but nonetheless Ligeia is the benefactor of the narrator, and when she dies he is her beneficiary. The situation is complicated by the fact that he, incredibly, cannot remember his wife's maiden name.

2. This quotation is from version K, in Thomas Ollive Mabbott, pages 336–37.

3. One example of an alive/dead beloved occurs in "The Sleeper." David Halliburton notices that the sleeper "is not an abiding spirit but a material presence on the threshold between life and death." He adds, wryly, "This creates a feeling of suspense that is not to everyone's taste" (45).

4. Mabbott notes that all four of these names denote "light" or "bright" (331).

5. Others have commented on Poe's macabre use of women in his poetry. For instance, Joan Dayan notices Poe's "interchangeable ladies" (*Fables* 126), though not in the context of signification. Leland Person sees Poe's women as not exactly interchangeable but as characters who work in the verse to express an "all-purpose ideal" (20).

6. J. Gerald Kennedy suggests that "Poe's variations upon the death-of-a-beautiful-woman paradigm enact the failure of language and the inconsolability of the writer" (76). I agree with Kennedy; Poe's signifiers of women enact a continual displacement that disparages correspondence and emphasizes difference.

7. Shoshana Felman, in discussing the signifying status of the purloined letter, sheds light on the status of women as signifiers, too: "For Lacan, what is repeated in the text is not the content of a fantasy but the symbolic displacement of a signifier through the insistence of a signifying chain: repetition is not of *sameness* but of *difference*, not of independent terms or of analogous themes but of a structure of differential interrelationships, in which what *returns* is always *other*" (147– 48).

8. In Hoffman's associative account of Poe, he suggests a somewhat similar reading of Poe: "To be the lover, or the would-be lover, of Annabel Lee, or Annabel Leigh, is a fate not easily avoided. On the one hand you end up yearning to lie down by her side in a sepulchre: necrophilia! On the other, you can't get her, can't get *at* her, can't consummate all those exacerbated urgings which you and she began to feel and which you haven't ever since ceased feeling, so you *incarnate* her in another" (23).

9. Lacan demonstrates the trickiness, the reversibility of some types of lying by offering the following joke:

"Why are you lying to me?" one character shouts breathlessly. "Yes, why do you lie to me saying you're going to Cracow so I should believe you're going to Lemberg, when in reality you *are* going to Cracow?" ("Seminar" 49)

10. Barbara Johnson observes how "contagious the deferment of the subject of the purloined letter can be" (111); Poe's speaker shares such contagion when it comes to the deferment of female signifiers.

11. Lacan further characterizes the unstable nature of the signifier as symbol of absence, asserting that "we cannot say of the purloined letter that, like other objects, it must be *or* not be in a particular place but that unlike them it will be *and* not be where it is, wherever it goes" (Seminar 54).

12. It anticipates, too, the lisping of Whitman's speaker in "Out of the Cradle," discussed in the next chapter.

13. Mabbott adds in a note: "Poe also believed that certain words or syllables in a line, because of repetition of sound or for some other reason, receive special emphasis. Here a natural reading is 'Of *poets*—by *poets*—as the *name*—is a *poet's*—*too*' " (391).

14. Mabbott notes the pun on the Spanish joke involving Ferdinando Mendez Pinto, famed for tall tales: "The name was regarded as a question and answer—'Mendez Ferdinando? Minto' means 'Ferdinand are you lying?—I lie.' When he admitted he was a liar he was not lying—and his name became a synonym for truth" (Mabbott 391).

CHAPTER 5: WORD, BIRTH, AND WHITMAN'S WATER CURE

1. Cayleff, though, sees a paradoxical conflating of autonomy and community in the attractions hydropathy offered: hydropathy appealed "not only to strains of individualism and personal advancement in American thought but also to gender-specific and culturally valued communal bonds, responsibility to others, and continuity in relationships; it offered a group context in which personal improvement could serve as a model for societal reformation" (17).

2. The underappreciated influence of Mary in the literature of nineteenth-century America is addressed by John Gatta, who states his argument as follows: "flirtation with the Marian cultus offered certain Protestant writers symbolic compensation for what might be culturally diagnosed as a deficiency of psychic femininity, or of anima, in America" (3).

3. In addition, the poem's repetition of the word "carols," used in conjunction with Christmas at least since the sixteenth century, according to the *Oxford English Dictionary*, makes less sense when the publishing history is neglected, but resonates when we consider that the word reinforces a connection with Christmas.

4. In this chapter, all poem citations are taken from Bradley and Blodgett, unless otherwise identified.

5. Christmas Eve heralds the immaculate birthing of a child from his mother, and eventually from this child, Jesus, comes the birth of the word as authorized by God. But we remain in a prepatriarchal mode in much of "Out of the Cradle."

6. Edwin Haviland Miller suggests that Whitman explores the child's first loss of the mother, just as the bird has abandoned her eggs in the nest (177).

7. Others have pointed to the similarities between "The Raven" and "Out of the Cradle." Betsy Erkkila, for example, notices the similarity of Whitman's speaker's cry of "Demon or bird!" to the cry of Poe's speaker, "bird or fiend" and also remarks that a sequence of Whitman's poem has "a Poesque ring" (173). At times the speaker of "Out of the Cradle," as in when he utters, "*O night! Do I not see my love fluttering out among the breakers?*" (249), becomes a Poe-like character, mourning the dead woman. Kenneth Price makes the valuable suggestion that although some critics believe Whitman echoed Poe, "it seems more likely that he intended to benefit from Poe's notoriety" (65).

8. The sea whispers, but also "lisps," a word that is a little disturbing, and resonates yet further with Poe-esque overtones. "Lisps" can have nonthreatening overtones, too, however: E.H. Miller points out that a mother lisps when she embraces her child; a child lisps when learning how to speak (184).

9. Other critics, notably Nathanson and Moon, have mentioned Whitman's connection with the Kristevan or Lacanian mother. Tenney Nathanson, for instance, discusses Kristeva and Whitman, including *chora*, as, for example, when he states that "it may be something of a paradox to suggest that Whitman's language, which is entoiled in representation, evokes a somatic state prior to the stabilization representation effects, a state structured instead as what Kristeva calls 'a pulsating *chora* . . . ,' " but that Kristeva suggests the pulsations can be found as "traces of infantile vocal behavior still present within adult language . . ." (126).

10. Of course Whitman does not use the word "signify" as Lacan does, but he does grapple with his own ideas of language theory. Warren points out that "scholarship of the last ten years indicates that 'the subject of language" occupied an important place in the literary culture of nineteenth-century America" (8). The Transcendentalists were interested in language not so much as communication but rather "as an expression of the spirit, whether individual or collective (Warren 12). Thurin even insists that Whitman had a *theory* of language (9). One of the major differences between Emerson's and Whitman's ideas of language inheres in Whitman's belief in language as the upwelling of a culture: "The idea of language as an unconscious expression of the national spirit is important for Whitman's theory of literature" (Warren 29). Interestingly, Bauerlein studies Whitman as a poet wishing "to overcome language, to fend off the possibility that words bear properties that cannot be reduced to human experience; the individual poems and pieces of criticism springing from that Orphic intention nevertheless register its dismemberment" (9).

11. Whitman is certainly capable at times of transgressing the feminine in a way that is aggressive, even rapacious. For example, in "A Woman Waits for Me" Whitman forces this awareness in a terrible rape sequence that results in impregnating his victim.

12. Whitman, the middle figure of the trio of poets considered here, catches up in his sea poems strains of Poe's "The Raven" and foretellings of Dickinson's "I

started Early—Took my Dog," all poems of endlessly rocking in womb pulsions, and attempting to return to the maternal in order to find voice that disrupts patriarchal naming. It would be fascinating to compare further Dickinson's "I started early" (P520), in which she uses a dog as her familiar, with Whitman's use of the bird as familiar. Her poem is a kind of bonzai version of Whitman's seascapes, "Out of the Cradle" and "As I Ebb'd."

CHAPTER 6: WORD, BIRTH, AND DICKINSON'S BOTANY TEXTS

1. Domhnall Mitchell makes this case thoroughly in his chapter, "Dickinson and Flowers," in *Emily Dickinson: Monarch of Perception*. For example, he states: "Emily Dickinson's writing on flowers serves as a valuable lens with which to look at political aspects of her poetry as a whole, but also at cultural ideology in the nineteenth century" (145).

2. There are also terms like lanceolate; both male terms and female sexual terms inhere, of course, in these botany texts (and I accentuate the female terms in my choices), though in regard to reproduction, the terms lean heavily toward the female.

3. While agreeing with many of Oberhaus's ideas of formatting in Dickinson's fascicles, I see the pith of my argument about Fascicle Twenty-Eight to be at odds with her argument about Fascicle Forty. She sees the Bible as Dickinson's ultimate authority, a dialogue with Jesus as containing exact and hopeful correspondence, and Jesus's House as being inviting to the speaker.

4. The presence of North makes it a doubly chilling poem. Wolff, referring to several poems using the word "North," including this one, posits that, "God's frigidity can even become perversely intermingled with the generative force that moves creation, 'Out of whose womb came the ice? and the hoary frost of heaven, who hath gendered it? The waters are hid as with a stone, and the face of the deep is frozen.' (Job 38: 29–30)" (314).

5. Porter, however, sees the ending of the poem somewhat differently than I do, stating that "Dickinson brings the poem into a triumphant Dantesque fusion of the self and creation. The ending stands out as a rare moment of high Emersonian transport" (161). Doriani sees the poem in the following terms: Dickinson apprehends God not as an absence "but as a powerful spiritual Presence" (74). Doriani understands Dickinson to see God as "both a distinct and personal being. What the speaker learns is that this being is also a faceless, invisible 'Infinitude'" (74). Interestingly, Doriani notes that "Dickinson rarely described direct encounters with God" and that this poem "is unusual in that sense" (75). My reading, in contradistinction to the two above, but along with Eberwein, concentrates more on the failure of language at the end of the poem.

6. I find instructive the transitive verb "pray," which includes legal definitions, as in petitioning the court. Such a legal denotation would have caught Dickinson's fancy, I think, as it offered a chance not only to test praying to her religious Father,

but also to her secular father, a lawyer, with the speaker needing to take on a courtroom politesse.

7. Mossberg offers a fascinating interpretation of this poem as stressing a "social and spiritual double-standard for boys and girls" (122); furthermore, the speaker "renounces prayer, and thus gives up her safe identity as 'little girl'" (126).

8. Eberwein argues that this poem "involves a child whose attempts to conform to the devotional practices she has been taught yield to independent application of golden-rule reasoning. Once she begins to think 'How prayer would feel—to—me—,' she stops bothering, or even insulting god by involving him in all her little problems" (256).

9. Sharon Cameron notes that the word variants that end many Dickinson poems almost function as poems in and of themselves.

10. Sewall discusses Lyon's serious efforts to convert her students to Christianity, dividing the school into "No-hopers" (Dickinson's group), "Hopers," and Christians; apparently Lyon and her teachers "kept fairly accurate track of the numbers in each group" (361).

11. In other poems of Fascicle Twenty-Eight we find lists—the alphabet and the words in the seventh poem, and the "Repealless—List" in the penultimate poem.

12. Gilbert and Gubar first noticed this tripartite division: God, father, husband.

13. Gilbert and Gubar, early on, saw the feminine possibilities for this poem: "Surely these 'strong Madonnas' are sisters of that mother Awe to whom, Dickinson told Higginson, she ran home as a child, and surely it was such mothers who enabled (and empowered) this poet to escape her Nobodaddy's requirements, if only in secret" (647).

14. In yet another summer poem, "All that is named of Summer Days/ Relinquished our Estate—" (1191), so that what is named is what is relinquished; the "Dams—of Ecstasy—" in the last line of this poem may connote a necessarily female aspect to ecstasy.

15. Harold Bloom identifies *apophrades* in his *Anxiety of Influence*, which he calls "return of the dead." With *apophrades*, time becomes inverted, so that the sensation created becomes that in which a forebear has been influenced by an inheritor.

16. The word "eider" magnetizes several meanings. As the down of the eider duck that stuffs the "Deep Pillow," in "My Life had stood—a Loaded Gun" (Fr764), it performs an important role in designating the relationship between the speaker and her "Owner": she provides for his comfort. The pillow, a Freudian figuring of the maternal breast, locates a female body image that gives further resonance to the idea that eider names are female nonnames. Eider names, the nameless names of the matronymic, persevere beneath the signifier, the world of the body and the maternal body in particular. Finally, the phrase "literature of misery" refers to women's literature of the nineteenth century, which takes its cue from the female eider duck who plucks feathers from her own breast to make her nest.

CONCLUSION: READING POETRY FROM ONE CENTURY TO ANOTHER

1. It is essential to think of homosexuality not simply as a preference or a behavior but as a culture and a linguistic unit; Harold Beaver, for instance, calls homosexuality a language (103). Such languages challenge Hegelian ways of conceptualizing the world, so that not everything, not even the most basic thing, we are beginning to understand, is composed of thesis and antithesis. Rather, compositions are a series of interactions that may or may not reference polarities at all. New distinctions of perceptions open up if we perceive an other as not simply opposite. If language is desire, too, and that desire is for an other, what then happens to the signifying chain? A rich world of slippage becomes available, and languages like homosexuality shuck off Hegelian antitheses by flooding them with new meaning.

2. Renza bases his claim for Poe's time-bombs on the play on the "French homonym 'demain' for the English 'domain' " (81) in "The Domain of Arnheim." Renza calls this Poe's "autobiographical 'interference,' his 'Kilroy was here' authorial traces, himself as the lost, absent cause of texts that, like those of his artistic peers, he foresees will indeed become 'lost causes' " (81).

3. Warren, interestingly, calls Whitman's ideal "athletic reading" in *Democratic Vistas*, a kind of reading dependent upon the body.

4. Though Whitman and Dickinson certainly rely upon the power of the body, it is worth restating that they also rely upon and never forget or verge too far from an awareness of the potential nihilism inherent in the universe. For Poe, too, as for them, there exists the material body but there also exists, in thrilling conjunction, the nothing. As illustration, Cavitch comments that, like Dickinson, Whitman "constantly glances ahead beyond the limits of personal experience to the abyss of death in which he finds no one at all in the emptiness: imagine there is nothing, he taunts himself, imagine there is no self" (71).

Works Cited

Bauerlein, Mark. *Whitman and the American Idiom*. Baton Rouge: Louisiana State UP, 1991.

Beaver, Harold. "Homosexual Signs." *Critical Inquiry* 8 (1981): 99–119.

Benfey, Christopher. *Emily Dickinson and the Problem of Others*. Amherst: U. of Massachusetts P, 1984.

Bennett, Paula. *Emily Dickinson: Woman Poet*. Iowa City: U of Iowa P, 1991.

Berg, Temma. "Suppressing the Language of Wo(Man): The Dream as a Common Language." *Engendering the Word: Feminist Essays in Psychosexual Poetics*. Ed. Temma Berg. Chicago: U of Illinois P, 1989. 3–28.

Blasing, Mutlu Konuk. *American Poetry: The Rhetoric of Its Forms*. New Haven, CT: Yale UP, 1987.

Bloom, Harold. *The Anxiety of Influence: A Theory of Poetry*. New York: Oxford UP, 1973.

Brodie, Janet Farrell. *Contraception and Abortion in Nineteenth-Century America*. Ithaca, NY: Cornell UP, 1994.

Burland, C. A. *The Arts of the Alchemists*. New York: Macmillan, 1967.

Burroughs, John. *The Writings of John Burroughs: Whitman: A Study*. Vol. X. Boston: Houghton Mifflin, 1904.

Cameron, Sharon. *Choosing Not Choosing: Dickinson's Fascicles*. Chicago: U of Chicago P, 1992.

Campbell, Joseph. *The Hero with a Thousand Faces*. Princeton, NJ: Princeton UP, 1968.

Capps, Jack L. *Emily Dickinson's Reading: 1836–1886*. Cambridge, MA: Harvard UP, 1966.

Caputi, Anthony. "The Refrain in Poe's Poetry." *On Poe: The Best from American Literature.* Eds. Louis J. Budd and Edwin H. Cady. Durham, NC: Duke UP, 1993. 92–101.

Carlson, Eric W., ed. *The Recognition of Edgar Allan Poe.* Ann Arbor: U of Michigan P, 1966.

Carpenter, Edward. *Some Friends of Walt Whitman: A Study in Sex-Psychology.* London: Athenaeum Press, 1924.

Carton, Evan. *The Rhetoric of American Romance: Dialectic and Identity in Emerson, Dickinson, Poe, and Hawthorne.* Baltimore, MD: Johns Hopkins UP, 1985.

"A Case of Childbirth, and Management of the New-Born Child." From the Editor's Notebook. *The Water-Cure Journal and Herald of Reforms.* June 29, 1847. Vol. VII, No. VI, New York: Fowler and Wells. 179–80.

Cavitch, David. *My Soul and I: The Inner Life of Walt Whitman.* Boston: Beacon, 1985.

Cayleff, Susan E. *Wash and Be Healed: The Water-Cure Movement and Women's Health.* Philadelphia: Temple UP, 1987.

Ceniza, Sherry. "'Being a Woman . . . I Wish to Give My Own View': Some Nineteenth-Century Women's Responses to the 1860 *Leaves of Grass.*" *The Cambridge Companion to Walt Whitman.* Ed. Ezra Greenspan. New York: Cambridge UP, 1995. 110–32.

———. *Walt Whitman and 19th-Century Women Reformers.* Tuscaloosa: U of Alabama P, 1998.

Cixous, Hélène. "The Laugh of the Medusa." *The Signs Reader: Women, Gender and Scholarship.* Ed. Elizabeth Abel and Emily K. Abel. Chicago: U of Chicago P, 1983. 279–97.

Cixous, Hélène, and Catherine Clement. *The Newly Born Woman.* Trans. Betsy Wing. Minneapolis: U of Minnesota P, 1975.

Clack, Randall A. *The Marriage of Heaven and Earth: Alchemical Regeneration in the Works of Taylor, Poe, Hawthorne, and Fuller.* Westport, CT: Greenwood Press, 2000.

Cooke, P. Pendleton. "Edgar A. Poe." *The Recognition of Edgar Allan Poe: Selected Criticism Since 1829.* Ed. Eric W. Carlson. Ann Arbor: U of Michigan P, 1969. 21–28.

Cowley, Malcolm. *Walt Whitman's Leaves of Grass: The First (1855) Edition.* New York: Penguin, 1985.

Crumbley, Paul. *Inflections of the Pen: Dash and Voice in Emily Dickinson.* Lexington: UP of Kentucky, 1997.

Danielson, Susan Steinberg. "Healing Women's Wrongs: Water-Cure as (Fictional) Autobiography." *Studies in the American Renaissance* (1992): 247–60.

Davidson, Edward H. *Poe: A Critical Study.* Cambridge: Belknap Press of Harvard UP, 1964.

Davidson, Michael. "'When the World Strips Down and Rouges Up': Redressing Whitman." *Breaking Bounds: Whitman and American Cultural Studies.* Eds. Betsy Erkkila and Jay Grossman. New York: Oxford UP, 1996. 220–237.

Dayan, Joan. "Amorous Bondage: Poe, Ladies, and Slaves." *The American Face of Edgar Allan Poe.* Eds. Shawn Rosenheim and Stephen Rachman. Baltimore: Johns Hopkins UP, 1995. 179–209.

———. *Fables of Mind: An Inquiry into Poe's Fiction.* New York: Oxford UP, 1987.

Debus, Allen G. "Renaissance Chemistry and the Work of Robert Fludd." *Alchemy and Chemistry in the Seventeenth Century.* Los Angeles: U of C, 1966. 1–29.

Degler, Carl. *At Odds: Women and the Family in America from the Revolution to the Present.* New York: Oxford UP, 1980.

Dickinson, Emily. *The Letters of Emily Dickinson.* Eds. Thomas H. Johnson and Theodora Ward. 3 vols. Cambridge, MA: Belknap P of Harvard UP, 1958.

———. *The Manuscript Books of Emily Dickinson.* Ed. R. W. Franklin. Cambridge, MA: Belknap P of Harvard UP, 1981.

———. *The Poems of Emily Dickinson.* Ed. R. W. Franklin. 3 vols. Cambridge, MA: Belknap P of Harvard UP, 1998.

———. *The Poems of Emily Dickinson.* Ed. Thomas H. Johnson. 3 vols. Cambridge, MA: Belknap P of Harvard UP, 1955.

D'israeli, Isaac. *Curiosities of Literature.* Ed. Everett Bleiler. New York, Dover, 1964.

Donegan, Jane B. *"Hydropathic Highway to Health": Women and Water-Cure in Antebellum America.* New York: Greenwood Press, 1986.

Doriani, Beth Maclay. *Emily Dickinson: Daughter of Prophecy.* Amherst: U of Massachusetts P, 1996.

Eberwein, Jane Donahue. *Dickinson: Strategies of Limitation.* Amherst: U of Massachusetts P, 1985.

Elmer, Jonathan. *Reading at the Social Limit: Affect, Mass Culture, and Edgar Allan Poe.* Stanford: Stanford UP, 1995.

Erkkila, Betsy. *Whitman the Political Poet.* New York: Oxford UP, 1989.

Felman, Shoshana. "On Reading Poetry: Reflections on the Limits and Possibilities of Psychoanalytic Approaches." *The Purloined Poe: Lacan, Derrida and Psychoanalytic Reading.* Eds. John P. Muller and William J. Richardson. Baltimore, MD: The Johns Hopkins UP, 1988. 133–56.

Fink, Bruce. *The Lacanian Subject: Between Language and Jouissance.* Princeton, NJ: Princeton UP, 1995.

Flax, Jane. "Signifying the Father's Desire: Lacan in a Feminist's Gaze." *Criticism and Lacan: Essays and Dialogue on Language, Structure, and the Unconscious.* Eds. Patrick Colm Hogan and Lalita Pandit. Athens: U of Georgia P, 1990. 109–19.

Fletcher, Richard M. *The Stylistic Development of Edgar Allan Poe.* Paris: Mouton, 1973.

Fone, Byrne. *Masculine Landscapes: Walt Whitman and the Homoerotic Text.* Carbondale: Southern Illinois UP, 1992.

Freud, Sigmund. "Beyond the Pleasure Principle." *The Standard Edition of the Complete Psychological Works of Sigmund Freud.* Ed. and Trans. James Strachey. London: The Hogarth Press, 1974. Vol. 18: 3.

Fuller, Margaret. "American Literature." *The Woman and the Myth: Margaret Fuller's Life and Writings*. Ed. Bell Gale Chevigny. Boston: Northeastern UP, 1994.

Gallop, Jane. *The Daughter's Seduction: Feminism and Psychoanalysis*. Ithaca, NY: Cornell UP, 1982.

————. *Reading Lacan*. Ithaca, NY: Cornell UP, 1985.

Garner, Shirley Nelson, Claire Kahane, and Madelon Sprengnether, Eds. "Introduction." *The (M)other Tongue: Essays in Feminist Psychoanalytic Interpretation*. Ithaca, NY: Cornell UP, 1985. 15–29.

Gatta, John. *American Madonna: Images of the Divine Woman in Literary Culture*. New York: Oxford UP, 1997.

Gilbert, Sandra, and Susan Gubar. *Madwoman in the Attic: The Woman Writer and the Nineteenth-Century Literary Imagination*. New Haven, CT: Yale UP, 1979.

Godwin, William. *Lives of the Necromancers. or, An Account of the Most Eminent Persons in Successive Ages, Who Have Claimed for Themselves, or to Whom Has Been Imputed by Others, The Exercise of Magical Power*. New York: Harper and Brothers, 1835.

Grabo, Norman S. *Edward Taylor*. Boston: G. K. Hall, 1988.

Greenspan, Ezra, ed. *The Cambridge Companion to Walt Whitman*. New York: Cambridge UP, 1995.

Grosz, Elizabeth. *Jacques Lacan: A Feminist Introduction*. New York: Routledge, 1990.

Halliburton, David. *Edgar Allan Poe: A Phenomenological View*. Princeton, NJ: Princeton UP, 1973.

Hayes, Kevin J. *Poe and the Printed Word*. New York: Cambridge UP, 2000.

Hoffman, Daniel. *Poe Poe Poe Poe Poe Poe Poe*. New York: Doubleday, 1972.

Homans, Margaret. "'Oh, Vision of Language!': Dickinson's Poems of Love and Death." *Feminist Critics Read Emily Dickinson*. Ed. Suzanne Juhasz. Bloomington: Indiana UP, 1983. 114–33.

Humphries, Jefferson. *Metamorphoses of the Raven: Literary Overdeterminedness in France and the South Since Poe*. Baton Rouge: Louisiana State UP, 1985.

Hutchinson, George. *The Ecstatic Whitman: Literary Shamanism and the Crisis of the Union*. Columbus: Ohio State UP, 1986.

Johnson, Barbara. *The Critical Difference: Essays in the Contemporary Rhetoric of Reading*. Baltimore: Johns Hopkins UP, 1958.

Kahn, Robbie Pfeufer. *Bearing Meaning: The Language of Birth*. Chicago: U of Illinois P, 1995.

Kamensky, Jane. *Governing the Tongue: The Politics of Speech in Early New England*. New York: Oxford UP, 1997.

Kaplan, Justin. *Walt Whitman: A Life*. New York: Simon and Schuster, 1980.

Kennedy, Gerald J. *Poe, Death, and the Life of Writing*. New Haven, CT: Yale UP, 1987.

Ketterer, David. The *Rationale of Deception in Poe*. Baton Rouge: Louisiana State University Press, 1979.

Killingsworth, M. Jimmie. *The Growth of Leaves of Grass: The Organic Tradition in Whitman Studies*. Columbia, SC: Camden House, 1993.

———. *Whitman's Poetry of the Body*. Chapel Hill: U of North Carolina P, 1989.

Kot, Paula. "Feminist Re-Visioning of the Tales of Women." *A Companion to Poe Studies*. Ed. Eric W. Carlson. Westport, CT: Greenwood Press, 1996. 388–402.

Kristeva, Julia. *Desire in Language: A Semiotic Approach to Literature and Art*. New York: Columbia UP, 1980.

———. *The Kristeva Reader*. Ed. Toril Moi. New York: Columbia UP, 1986.

———. *Revolution in Poetic Language*. Trans. Margaret Waller. New York: Columbia UP, 1984.

Lacan, Jacques. "Desire and the Interpretation of *Hamlet*." *Yale French Studies* 55/56 (1977): 11–52.

———. *Écrits*. Paris: Editions du Seuil, 1966.

———. *Écrits: A Selection*. Trans. Alan Sheridan. New York: Norton, 1977.

———. *Feminine Sexuality*. Ed. Juliet Mitchell and Jacqueline Rose. Trans. Jacqueline Rose. New York: Norton, 1982.

———. "Seminar on 'The Purloined Letter.'" Trans. Jeffrey Mehlman. *Yale French Studies* 48 (1972): 39–72.

Lambert, Robert. *Emily Dickinson's Use of Anglo-American Legal Concepts and Vocabulary in Her Poetry*. Lewiston: Edwin Mellen, 1997.

Larson, Kerry. *Whitman's Drama of Consensus*. Chicago: U of Chicago P, 1988.

Leverenz, David. "Poe and Gentry Virginia." *The American Face of Edgar Allan Poe*. Eds. Shawn Rosenheim and Stephen Rachman. Baltimore: Johns Hopkins UP, 1995. 210–36.

Lincoln, Mrs. Almira H. *Familiar Lectures on Botany, Practical, Elementary, and Physiological with an Appendix containing Descriptions of The Plants of the United States and Exotics, &c*. New York: Huntington and Savage, 1845.

Ljungquist, Kent. *The Grand and the Fair: Poe's Landscape Aesthetics and Pictorial Techniques*. Potomac, MI: Scripta Humanistica, 1984.

Loeffelholz, Mary. *Dickinson and the Boundaries of Feminist Theory*. Chicago: U of Illinois P, 1991.

Loving, Jerome. *Emily Dickinson: The Poet on the Second Story*. Cambridge: Cambridge UP, 1986.

Lowenberg, Carlton. *Emily Dickinson's Textbooks*. Lafayette, CA: West Coast Print Center, 1986.

Luker, Kristin. *Abortion and the Politics of Motherhood*. Berkeley: U of California P, 1984.

Mallonee, Barbara C. "Leaving Latitude: Emily Dickisnon and Indian Pipes." *The Georgia Review* (1999): 223–44.

Martin, Robert K. "Whitman and the Politics of Identity." *Walt Whitman: The Centennial Essays*. Ed. Ed Folsom. Iowa City: U of Iowa P, 1994. 172–81.

Matthiessen, F.O. *American Renaissance: Art and Empression in the Age of Emerson and Whitman*. New York: Oxford UP, 141.

Meyers, Jeffrey. *Edgar Allan Poe: His Life and Legacy*. New York: Scribner, 1992.

Michie, Helena. *The Flesh Made Word: Female Figures and Women's Bodies*. New York: Oxford, 1987.

Miller, Christanne. *Emily Dickinson: A Poet's Grammar*. Cambridge: Harvard UP, 1987.

Miller, Edwin Haviland. *Walt Whitman's Poetry*. Boston: Houghton Mifflin, 1968.

Miller, James E. *The American Quest for a Supreme Fiction*. Chicago: U of Chicago P, 1979.

——— . *Walt Whitman's Poetry: A Psychological Journey*. Boston: Houghton Mifflin, 1968.

Mitchell, Domhnall. *Emily Dickinson: Monarch of Perception*. Amherst: U of Massachusetts P, 2000.

Moi, Toril. *Sexual/Textual Politics: Feminist Literary Theory*. New York: Methuen, 1985.

Moon, Michael. *Disseminating Whitman: Revision and Corporeality in Leaves of Grass*. Cambridge, MA: Harvard UP, 1991.

Mossberg, Barbara Antonina Clarke. *Emily Dickinson: When a Writer Is a Daughter*. Bloomington: Indiana UP, 1982.

Muller, John P., and William J. Richardson. *Lacan and Language: A Reader's Guide to Écrits*. New York: International Universities Press, 1982.

——— . *The Purloined Poe: Lacan, Derrida and Psychoanalytic Reading*. Baltimore: Johns Hopkins UP, 1988.

Murray, Barbara. "The *Scarlet Experiment*: Emily Dickinson's Abortion Experience." Dissertation. Knoxville: U of Tennessee, December 1988. (Dir. William Shurr)

Nathanson, Tenney. *Whitman's Presence: Body, Voice, and Writing in Leaves of Grass*. New York: New York UP, 1992.

Nolan, James. *Poet-Chief: The Native American Poetics of Walt Whitman and Pablo Neruda*. Albuquerque: U of New Mexico P, 1994.

Oberhaus, Dorothy Huff. *Emily Dickinson's Fascicles: Method and Meaning*. University Park: Pennsylvania State UP, 1995.

Olney, James. *The Language(s) of Poetry: Walt Whitman, Emily Dickinson, Gerard Manley Hopkins*. Athens: U of Georgia P, 1993.

Osgood, Frances S. *The Poetry of Flowers and Flowers of Poetry*. Philadelphia: Lippincott, 1864.

Ostriker, Alicia. *Stealing the Language: The Emergence of Women's Poetry in America*. Boston: Beacon P, 1986.

Payne, Michael. *Reading Theory: An Introduction to Lacan, Derrida, and Kristeva*. Cambridge: Blackwell, 1993.

Person, Leland. *Aesthetic Headaches: Women and a Masculine Poetics in Poe, Melville, and Hawthorne*. Athens: U of Georgia P, 1988.

Phillips, Elizabeth. "The Poems: 1824–1835." *A Companion to Poe Studies*. Ed. Eric W. Carlson. Westport, CT: Greenwood Press, 1996. 67–88.

Plath, Sylvia. *The Collected Poems*. Ed. Ted Hughes. New York: Harper & Row, 1981.

Poe, Edgar Allan. *Collected Works of Edgar Allan Poe*. Ed. Thomas Ollive Mabbott. Vol. I: Poems. Cambridge: Belknap P of Harvard UP, 1969.

————. *Essays and Reviews*. Ed. G. R. Thompson. New York: The Library of American, 1984.

————. *The Fall of the House of Usher and Other Writings: Poems, Tales, Essays and Reviews*. Ed. David Galloway. New York: Penguin, 1985.

Pollak, Vivian R. *Dickinson: The Anxiety of Gender*. Ithaca, NY: Cornell UP, 1984.

————. *The Erotic Whitman*. Berkeley: U of California P, 2000.

————. "'In Loftiest Spheres': Whitman's Visionary Feminism." *Breaking Bounds: Whitman and American Cultural Studies*. Eds. Betsy Erkkila and Jay Grossman. New York: Oxford UP, 1996. 92–111.

Porter, David. *Dickinson: The Modern Idiom*. Cambridge, MA: Harvard UP, 1981.

Price, Kenneth. *Whitman and Tradition: The Poet in His Century*. New Haven, CT: Yale UP, 1990.

Quinn, Patrick R. *The French Face of Edgar Poe*. Carbondale: Southern Illinois UP, 1957.

Ragland-Sullivan, Ellie, and Mark Bracher, eds. *Lacan and the Subject of Language*. New York: Routledge, 1991.

Read, John. *Prelude to Chemistry: An Outline of Alchemy, Its Literature and Relationships*. New York: Macmillan, 1937.

Redgrove, H. Stanley. *Alchemy: Ancient and Modern*. New York: University Books, 1969.

Renza, Louis A. "Poe's Secret Autobiography." *The American Renaissance Reconsidered*. Eds. Walter Benn Michaels and Donald E. Pease. Baltimore: Johns Hopkins UP, 1985. 58–89.

Reynolds, David S. *Beneath the American Renaissance: The Subversive Imagination in the Age of Emerson and Melville*. New York: Knopf, 1988.

————. *Walt Whitman's America: A Cultural Biography*. New York: Knopf, 1995.

Richard, Claude. "The Heart of Poe and the Rhythmics of the Poems." *Critical Essays on Edgar Allan Poe*. Ed. Eric W. Carlson. Boston: G. K. Hall, 1987. 195–206.

Riddel, Joseph. "The 'Crypt' of Edgar Poe." *Boundary 2: A Journal of Postmodern Literature*. 7:3 (1979): 117–44.

Riley, Denise. *"Am I That Name?": Feminism and the Category of "Women" in History*, Minneapolis: U of Minnesota P, 1988.

Roberts, Gareth. *The Mirror of Alchemy: Alchemical Ideas and Images in Manuscripts and Books from Antiquity to the Seventeenth Century*. Toronto: U of Toronto P, 1994.

Salska, Agnieszka. *Walt Whitman and Emily Dickinson: Poetry of the Central Consciousness*. Philadelphia: U of Pennsylvania P, 1985.

Saltz, Laura. "'(Horrible to Relate!)': Recovering the Body of Marie Rogêt." *The American Face of Edgar Allan Poe*. Eds. Shawn Rosenheim and Stephen Rachman. Baltimore: The Johns Hopkins UP, 1995. 237–67.

Schneiderman, Stuart. "Fictions." *Lacan and the Subject of Languge*. Eds. Ellie Ragland- Sullivan and Mark Bracher. New York: Routledge, 1991. 152–66.

Sewall, Richard. *The Life of Emily Dickinson*. 2 vols. New York: Farrar, Straus and Giroux, 1974.

Shurr, William H. *The Marriage of Emily Dickinson: A Study of the Fascicles*. Lexington: UP of Kentucky, 1983.

Silverman, Kenneth. *Edgar A. Poe: Mournful and Never-Ending Remembrance*. New York: HarperCollins, 1991.

Smith, Martha Nell. *Rowing in Eden: Rereading Emily Dickinson*. Austin: U of Texas P, 1992.

Smith, Robert McClure. *The Seductions of Emily Dickinson*. Tuscaloosa: U of Alabama P, 1996.

Smith, Stephanie. *Conceived by Liberty: Maternal Figures in Nineteenth-Century American Literature*. Ithaca, NY: Cornell UP, 1994.

Smith-Rosenberg, Carroll. *Disorderly Conduct: Visions of Gender in Victorian America*. New York: Knopf, 1985.

Stoehr, Taylor. "'Unspeakable Horror' in Poe." *The South Atlantic Quarterly* 78 (Summer 1979): 317–32.

Stoltzfus, Ben. *Lacan and Literature: Puloined Pretexts*. Albany: SUNY P, 1996.

Stovall, Floyd. *Edgar Poe the Poet*. Charlottesville: UP of Virginia, 1969.

Thorpe, Dwayne. "The Poems: 1836–1849." *A Companion to Poe Studies*. Ed. Eric W. Carlson. Westport, CT: Greenwood Press, 1996. 89–109.

Thurin, Erik Ingvar. *Whitman between Impressionism and Expressionism: Language of the Body, Language of the Soul*. Lewisburg, PA: Bucknell UP, 1995.

Traubel, Horace, ed. *An American Primer*. Boston: Small, Maynard, 1904.

Tufariello, Catherine. "'The Remembering Wine': Emerson's Influence on Whitman and Dickinson." *The Cambridge Companion to Ralph Waldo Emerson*. Ed. Joel Porte and Saundra Morris. New York: Cambridge UP, 1999. 162–91.

Wardrop, Daneen. *Emily Dickinson's Gothic: Goblin with a Gauge*. Iowa City: U of Iowa P, 1996.

Warren, James Perrin. *Walt Whitman's Language Experiment*. University Park: Pennsylvania State UP, 1990.

Webster, Noah. *An American Dictionary of the English Language*. 2 vols. New York: S. Converse, 1828.

Weisbuch, Robert. *Atlantic Double Cross: American Literature and British Influence in the Age of Emerson*. Chicago: U of Chicago P, 1986.

Werner, Marta L. *Dickinson's Open Folios: Scenes of Reading, Surfaces of Writing*. Ann Arbor: U of Michigan P, 1995.

Whelan, Carol Zapata. "'Do I Contradict Myself?': Progression through Contraries in Walt Whitman's 'The Sleepers.'" *Walt Whitman Quarterly Review* 10: 1 (Summer 1992): 25–39.

Whicher, George Frisbie. *This Was a Poet: A Critical Biography of Emily Dickinson*. New York: Scribner's, 1938.

Whitman, Walt. *The Collected Writings of Walt Whitman: A Textual Variorum of the Printed Poem*. Vol. II, 1860–1867. Eds. Sculley Bradley, Harold W. Blodgett, Arthur Golden, and William White. New York: New York UP, 1980.

———. *Leaves of Grass*. Eds. Sculley Bradley and Harold Blodgett. New York: Norton, 1973.

———. *Leaves of Grass*. Ed. Malcolm Cowley. New York: Penguin, 1985.

Williams, Michael J. S. *A World of Words: Language and Displacement in the Fiction of Edgar Allan Poe*. Durham, NC: Duke UP, 1988.

Wolff, Cynthia Griffin. *Emily Dickinson*. New York: Alfred A. Knopf, 1986.

Wolosky, Shira. *Emily Dickinson: A Voice of War*. New Haven, CT: Yale UP, 1984.

Wood, Alphonso. *A Class-Book of Botany, Designed for Colleges, Academies, and Other Seminaries Where the Science is Taught* . . . Boston: Crocker and Brewster, 1845.

Zayed, Georges. *The Genius of Edgar Allan Poe*. Rochester, VT: Schenkman Books, 1985.

Index

About the Author

DANEEN WARDROP is Associate Professor of English at Western Michigan University. She is the author of *Emily Dickinson's Gothic: Goblin with a Gauge* (1996) and her articles have appeared in such journals as *Texas Studies in Literature and Language, ESQ, African American Review,* and *The Emily Dickinson Journal.*